MW01025677

MEN AND WOMEN

Gender, Judaism and Democracy

MEN AND WOMEN

Gender, Judaism and Democracy

EDITOR:

RACHEL ELIOR

מכון ון ליר בירושלים
THE VAN LEER JERUSALEM INSTITUTE
معهد فان لير في القدس

URIM PUBLICATIONS
Jerusalem • New York

Men and Women: Gender, Judaism and Democracy
Edited by Rachel Elior

Translated from the Hebrew *Rav Goni* (volume III) by Shmuel Sermoneta-Gertel.
Printed at Hemed Press, Israel.
First Edition.

ISBN 965-7108-54-3

The Van Leer Jerusalem Institute, P.O. Box 4070, Jerusalem 91040, Israel
www.vanleer.org.il

Lambda Publishers, Inc.
3709 13th Avenue, Brooklyn, New York 11218 USA
Tel: 718-972-5449 Fax: 718-972-6307 mh@ejudaica.com
Urim Publications, P.O. Box 52287, Jerusalem 91521 Israel
www.UrimPublications.com

CONTENTS

Socio-Religious Encounters in the Past

The Educational Process from a Gender Perspective

Introduction

RACHEL ELIOR

For thousands of years, from ancient times until the 20th century, written Jewish culture was created exclusively by men. They were its creators, its students, its interpreters and its teachers – as clearly witnessed by the fact that the Hebrew terms *"tana"* (scholar of the mishnaic period), *"hakham"* (sage/rabbi), *"rav"* (rabbi), *"posek"* (halakhic authority), *"dayan"* (rabbinical court judge), *"moreh halak-hah"* (rabbi/halakhic authority) have no equivalent in the feminine; and as evidenced by the fact that there is not one book in the Hebrew language, written, edited or published by a woman within the confines of the traditional world. The situation in the contemporary religious world – whereby women are barred from the *yeshiva*, the study hall and the *kolel* (*yeshivah* for married men), and have little or no voice in the rabbinical court, the synagogue, or in public affairs – clearly reflects the disparity between the sexes in the past and in the present. Torah study, the central value in the Jewish world, was the exclusive province of men; and *Halakhah* and other writings in the traditional world – which reflect the male perspective – have no female equivalent.

In the millennia-old literary tradition of the "People of the Book," not a single book written by a woman, or reflecting a woman's point of view, appeared before the late 19th to early 20th century. This silence is no coincidence. It is the product of a complex reality in which differences of destiny, rights and status, as well as the extent of sovereignty, freedom and equality, were all extrapolated from biological differences. This reality forced all women into a patriarchal order, in which they were denied sovereignty – as their fathers' and husbands' possessions, and confined as they were to the realm of home and family and barred from all public activity.

By excluding women from public life, this approach has prevented them from taking part in study, culture and creativity, leadership and law, since all of these things require freedom of movement, independence and sovereignty, education and a place in the public domain. The boundary between within and without, the private and the public domains, subjugation and sovereignty, was also the boundary between silence and anonymity on the one hand, and a voice – the power of the spoken and the written word – on the other. Subjugating and excluding patriarchalism was an integral part of many cultures, and determined the fate of most women throughout history, although each culture explained and justified it in keeping with its own values, and rooted in its holy scriptures. For eons, the fate of women was characterized by discrimination, exclusion and forced silence – until the 20th century brought change in the status of women, and recognition of their right to equality, sovereignty and education.

These rights often clash with various traditional approaches, fostering discussion of such subjects as women's study, the status of women, women in traditional texts, and changes in consciousness and *Halakhah* – in light of the past. The mores of the past, created within the patriarchal religious world, affect the status of women in all communities. Discourse between the various communities – conducted from a variety of viewpoints, and addressing common issues, a new consciousness and the fostering of dialogue – serves to build new bridges between the past and the present.

Modern liberal society – founded upon principles of freedom; equal rights; the amendment of laws and government, on the basis of considered criticism; pluralism; and inherent human dignity – has presented alternatives to the traditional patriarchal order, promoting equal rights between the sexes in legislation, education and equal access to sources of authority and knowledge. It has also created new opportunities for participation in culture, law, science and the arts, unknown before the 20th century. At the same time however, the stamp of patriarchalism still remains in many areas: from the Hebrew language, which expresses relationships between men and women in terms of ownership; through the personal status laws, based upon a religious legal system that fails to recognize equality between the sexes, and religious ritual performed entirely by men; to entire academic and professional fields still closed to women, for various reasons. Relations between the sexes entail dialogue between sacred tradition and democratic culture, and concern many different issues in the realm of authority and change, balance of power, ownership and sovereignty, ideology and family, law and education, modesty and exclusion, the authority of single-gender leadership, and many other questions pertaining to the foundations of the social order and relations between men and women.

The conference on "Men and Women: Gender, Judaism and Democracy," held in July 1998, was devoted to the changing meanings of gender reality within Israeli culture. Contemporary society as a whole is heir to the patriarchal order – *nolens volens* – since a considerable part of language, culture, law and custom preserve this order. Patriarchalism is rooted in the traditional world which, for a large proportion of the Israeli public is sacrosanct and its values timeless, while others claim it requires re-evaluation and adaptation to the changing times. Various approaches and voices can be heard on the subject: Some wish to maintain the patriarchal order as is, perpetuating male prerogative and female inferiority, based on the claim that essential differences warrant different rights; others demand segregation between men and women in various areas of religious and secular life, establishing a separate system of rights and obligations for each; and yet others believe that the components of the traditional order should be re-examined, in light of humanistic thought and egalitarian criticism – advocating equal rights for all.

Like any historical phenomenon, the traditional world – which derives its authority from the past, and legitimacy from *Halakhah* and custom – does not stand in one place, isolated from its environment. It evolves over time, relating to continuity and change, the force of *Halakhah*, new ideas, and the surrounding consciousness and reality. Nor does the modern world hold a single position and a fixed set of values, but rather changes constantly in its relationship with the past, from which it derives language, culture and tradition; and in its relationship with the present, which it fashions through the power of changing experience and new ideas that constantly raise the issue of real versus ideal, precedent versus innovation and criticism.

The aim of this collection is to approach, from the perspective of gender: the complex interaction between shared and distinct values within the mesh of Judaism and democracy; between sacred traditional values and contemporary values; and between prevailing norms rooted in the past, and changing consciousness.

At the heart of the discussion, lie relations between men and women – founded upon religious law, traditional reality and secular criticism, ancient custom and changing reality, modern law and humanistic standards, equal rights and differences in status and destiny, dominant and silent voices in the past and present. The contributors, both men and women, differ from one another in their lifestyles and in their level of commitment to respective cultural, religious and legal values, but all take part in the renewed reading of changing reality in religious and secular society, and in examining relations between society's component parts and the sources of its identity and identification.

The legacies of the past are examined from different perspectives. There are those who take a critical approach toward *Halakhah*, and those who seek to deconstruct male cultural language, reconstructing it to express the "new" women's experience, alongside the "old," dominant male voice. There are those who strive to penetrate the various historical strata, in order to rescue lost voices and shed light on marginalized alternatives, while others seek to gain feminine insight into the traditional texts, releasing them from exclusive male control. Among those who return to the past and its precedents, re-examining the different voices it comprises, and among the commentators and critics, scholars and readers – some favor appropriating tradition and adopting the male cultural language, while others aspire to create a new female language, alongside the prevailing traditional male language, offering alternative concepts in the fields of social values and legal interpretation. The many voices present in this collection clearly demonstrate the existence of a new dialogue, re-examining the past, as well as shaping the present and the future.

The conference aroused a great deal of interest. The atmosphere in many of the sessions was intense, at times even tension-filled and impassioned – reflecting the feeling shared by all participants, men and women alike, that they were taking part in a decisive moment of change. The status of women in Israel, in the traditional and modern worlds, is an emotionally charged subject, presently at a number of crossroads. Consequently, the various approaches reflect frustration, criticism, expectations of change of consciousness, doubts, and debates, as well as hopes. The various lectures and points of view presented, made it eminently clear that gender-related questions pertaining to Judaism and democracy lie at the heart of discourse within the different communities – some committed to *Halakhah*, and some espousing other value systems, stressing equality and partnership, humanism and feminism, to which few are indifferent, and regarding which many wish to voice their opinion. Following the conference, a discussion group was established, to address the issue of dialogue between men and women in the traditional world and in modern society. The group continued to pursue careful analysis of the various topics raised during the conference.

The participants, both men and women, from a variety of fields, maintaining different beliefs and lifestyles, are all part of the ongoing dialogue between tradition and progress and between Judaism and democracy, conducted under the auspices of The Framework for Contemporary Jewish Thought and Identity at the Van Leer Jerusalem Institute.

The collection comprises eleven articles, in four different areas: The Law: Patriarchy and Equality; Past and Present: History and Culture from a Gender Perspective; Socio-Religious Encounter in the Past; The Educational Process from a Gender Perspective.

The Law: Patriarchy and Equality

Pinhas Shifman examines the family status of women from the perspective of the Israeli legal system, which is marked by a duality between religious-halakhic law in matters of marriage and divorce, and secular-civil law in matters of child-support, custody and property. This duality is further enhanced by the patriarchal world view espoused by *Halakhah*, in contrast to equality-oriented civil law. The author raises the issue of a rabbinical court system that ignores the prevailing reality, which has internalized values of partnership and equality in marriage; and takes a look at the predilection toward patriarchal values that reinforce the traditional family structure.

Orit Kamir discusses the legal meaning of human dignity, a new concept in Israeli legal parlance, created as a result of the refusal by religious and *haredi* factions in the Knesset to afford constitutional status to the value of equality. According to Israeli law, women are not entitled to equality in their family lives, since they are subject to religious law, which does not recognize this value. The legal status afforded to human dignity helps to improve the status of women in places where attempts to rely on the value of equality have encountered difficulties. The article examines the change that has taken place over the past two decades regarding the legal and social meaning of women's dignity and its changing application.

Susan Weiss addresses the injustice and inequality between men and women, stemming from the laws of marriage and divorce, which are based on biblical law and its halakhic interpretation. The author points out the fact that according to Israeli law, the personal status of married women is entirely at their husbands' discretion, since a woman does not have the right to divorce without her husband's consent. The husband's right to divorce his wife, however, is not dependent upon her consent. The article calls for a new interpretation of *Halakhah*, based on a commitment to correct this injustice.

Deborah Weissman reviews the positions taken by Rabbi Kook and Rabbi Uziel on the issue of women's suffrage, and looks into the halakhic ramifications concerning women's political activity today. A woman's right to vote and be elected to various institutions is one of the central issues of gender, religion and democracy. A look at halakhic positions associating modesty and violation of traditional values with the prohibition against women taking part in public life, sheds light on the entire issue of the status of women in the public domain. The author presents two opposing positions and their halakhic and social background, in an attempt to re-

15

examine the concept of "public dignity" today. Women are denied the right to vote and be elected to various public institutions in both the religious and secular world.

Past and Present: History and Culture from a Gender Perspective

Rachel Elior discusses the social and cultural significance of the exclusion of women from institutions of learning, jurisprudence and leadership in the traditional world. Exclusion from the public arena, rooted in written law and detailed in hallowed literary tradition, prevented women from taking part in shaping the norms that governed their lives and made them inferior in status, devoid of sovereignty, and subjugated to male authority. This limited existence, the essence of which is subjection to male ownership in connection with childbearing and service, is reflected in the fact that not a single book in the Hebrew language was written, edited or published by a woman in the traditional world, until the 20th century. The article deals with the foundations of the patriarchal order, based on inequality between members of different groups, examining the religious language in which it is rooted and the cultural tradition that derives from it.

Lea Shakdiel explains the connection between Jewish feminism and *tikkun ha-olam* ("repairing the world"), demanding that the female half of the population be given equal opportunity to participate in the struggle to fulfill the liberal-humanist vision – characterized by socio-ethical protest, striving for a more just society, and treating weaker groups justly and kindly. The author discusses feminism of gender difference, based on the equal value assigned to different roles and unique cultural contributions. Shakdiel associates this position with *tikkun ha-olam* inspired by a feminist approach, advocating morality of compassion and ethos of coop-eration, and expanding the "the world" to be repaired, by adding feminist goals to the repertoire of traditional "*tikkun.*"

Chana Safrai addresses the tension that exists within a society that internalizes the egalitarian democratic principle, yet see itself as part of an opposing religious framework that excludes women. This duality is characteristic of both religious-Zionist and secular society – which is bound to religious institutions. Safrai evaluates the legitimacy of full participation by women in prayer, based on the halakhic framework, which includes various options. The discus-sion focuses on currently accepted exclusion of women – which has ceased to be accepted in terms of western values – in light of the alternatives that appear upon closer examination of the histori-cal development of *Halakhah*.

Socio-Religious Encounter in the Past

Tova Cohen examines the first conscious attempt by women to cross the high gender barrier between women and the Hebrew language in traditional society, which forced women to live in ignorance of the canonical texts and the language of high culture. This attempt to effect change in the cultural status of Jewish women should be seen in light of the prevailing view that intellec-tual activities were the exclusive province of men. A small number of women, who obtained a Hebrew education in the second half of the 19th century and saw themselves as part of the *Haskalah* movement, marked the beginning of change in the place of women in the new Hebrew cultural world. This change, characterized by familiarity with the Hebrew language, grammar and traditional texts – and their personal appropriation – was the beginning of Hebrew women's writing, and modern women's Jewish scholarship.

Naftali Rothenberg takes a look at the reaction in male Jewish writings to discrimination against women, and their exclusion in public and private life. He asks whether these works reflect agreement and compliance with the gender reality of the writers' times, or perhaps a desire to challenge and change. The author perceives challenge and change in three areas: in halakhic criticism of polygamous norms and the establishment of monogamy as a counter-ideal; in emphasizing love and relations between the sexes as an expression of perfection, and reciprocity as a counterweight to discrimination-based hierarchy; and in the development of gender theology in kabbalistic literature, offering a female element alongside the male, in its perceptions of the soul and divinity.

The Educational Process from a Gender Perspective

Bilha Admanit addresses relations between men and women in terms of majority and minority, regarding the quality and concentration of power. Admanit claims that members of minority groups build self and group identity through interaction with the majority identity, seeking to build significant identification with the group. The discussion focuses on three ways in which a minority may act vis-à-vis the majority: rejecting majority norms, and setting itself apart; eliminating its unique character, and attempting to assimilate; and developing that which is unique, making it a part of the accepted norm, striving to achieve equality and legitimate participation in the social process. The challenge to education lies in fostering dialogue in which there is equality of value even without equality of identity, in the spirit of the third option, and in developing a different voice.

Chana Kehat discusses feminism within Orthodoxy, noting four types of women's behavior: sacrifice for the sake of male spiritual fulfillment – the prevailing model in *haredi* and national-*haredi* circles; women's scholarship in Modern Orthodox circles; militant feminism, prevalent in American Modern Orthodoxy; and female existence without voice or status – common in circles where the traditional patriarchal order prevails. The article compares the guiding principles of the different groups, and discusses differences in the development of feminist consciousness in various circles in Israel and in the Diaspora, and the accompanying differences in religious commitment. The various groups have different study and education patterns, affecting their respective approaches to male hegemony, and new demands concerning participation in ritual, rabbinical leadership and communal responsibility.

This collection is not a sealed scholarly work, presenting final research conclusions, but rather a many-voiced discourse seeking to present different viewpoints on the relationship between ideal and reality in a changing world, its roots, values, customs and parameters, in the context of gender. Some of the participants have striven to effect change, some have focused on the factual presentation of a certain topic, and some have expressed their feelings on the gap between ideal and reality. Some of the authors have chosen to adopt a subjective position, since they themselves are part of the society they wish to change, while maintaining its values and identifying with its essence in other areas. Others have taken an objective position, describing reality from a professional perspective, looking in from the outside and analyzing its complexity with critical empathy.

I would like to thank all of the members of the steering committee of The Framework for Contemporary Jewish Thought and Identity, who have participated in the ongoing dialogue between diverse points of view, and who have organized the conferences, designed to increase understanding of that which divides us, as well as that which unites us. I thank the Framework's directors, Professor Eliezer Schweid and Professor Naftali Rothenberg, and Van Leer Director Dr. Shimshon Zelniker. Special thanks to those who have worked throughout the year in organizing the conference, particularly Rabbi Chashi Freedman and Yona Ratzon, and to all who have taken part in pursuing the various avenues raised during the course of discussion. Thank you to Sara Soreni, in charge of editing and publishing *Ravgoni*, and to Felix Posen and the Posen Foundation, who have provided support for the translation and distribution of the collection. The Van Leer Jerusalem Institute, its administration and employees are a valuable resource in deepening inter-cultural dialogue in Israel, and in extending it in new directions. For that they have earned the gratitude of all who participated in the conference, as well as the readers of this printed version of its sessions.

The Law

Patriarchy and Equality

The Family Status of Women: Legal Changes and Social Climate

PINHAS SHIFMAN

The family status of women, from an Israeli legal perspective, suffers from the prevailing duality between religious and secular law. Marriage and divorce are subject to religious law, while matters pertaining to property relations between the partners – alimony and children – may be decided in family court, according to civil law. At first sight, one can discern different voices and contradictory messages emanating from the legal system. On the one hand, religious law represents a patriarchal view of the family, whereby the man is the provider, and the woman is in charge of the children and the household. Civil law on the other hand, declares its goal of achieving equality between the sexes, despite its inability to influence the religious laws governing marriage and divorce. The religious perspective is heightened by the role of the religious courts, the authority of which is determined however by the secular legislature. Battles over jurisdiction and authority thus express the desire of each perspective to increase its sphere of influence at the expense of the other.

At second glance however, it appears that we should avoid approaching the issue of women in the family solely from a static point of view. We must examine the problems involved not only based upon prevailing norms, but taking a dynamic perspective as well, considering their capacity for change. The secret of revolution lies in its ability to adapt symbols from the past to changing reality, i.e., to continue to use them, but to imbue them with new meaning. The words of Rabbi Kook "the old will be renewed and the new will be sanctified" (*Igrot HaRAY"aH*, 1, 164, p. 214), expresses a similar view, seeking to apply values and symbols from the past to the innovations of the present.

In this, scientific research – which seeks to place ideas in their historical and textual context – differs greatly from creative *midrashic* interpretation, which strives to break new ground, even at the cost of taking symbols and ideas out of their original context, associating them with new contexts. Careful scientific examination can also help us to confine ideas to their historical context, allowing them to sink deeply in their place, without serving as a model for the future. Thus for example, when approaching the sources of Jewish religious law in a given case, we must ask whether they represent an inviolable principle, or perhaps reflect social circumstances that were appropriate in their time, and as such, possess the potential for normative change as a result of fundamental changes within society. Since I will be focusing primarily on the legal aspect, I will make only brief references to religious law – requiring further development and elaboration.

The verse "the king's daughter is all glorious within" (Ps. 45:14) is often used to express the idea that the natural, honorable and suitable place for a woman is in the home. Those who cite this phrase however, are little aware of the fact that it is often interpreted in rabbinic literature in a manner critical of women. In the tractate of *Eruvin* (100b), we find among the curses suffered by Eve: a woman is "swathed like a mourner, ashamed to go out with head uncovered"; "outcast by men [...] forbidden to all but her husband, while men may take many wives"; "imprisoned: the king's daughter is all glorious within." [Rashi]

What is usually cited as a blessing is seen here as an expression of the lack of equality between men and women and as a curse, reflected in the socio-cultural reality of the day, considered to be a product of women's nature. *Halakhah* conformed to reality, which it perceived as shameful and cursed rather than praiseworthy and blessed.

With regard to the other side of the coin – that of men going forth – it is worth noting that the tent, as a metaphor for the study hall (in the sense of "giving up one's life in the tent of the Torah"), is a clearly female domain. Also worth noting is the perception that Torah study saps a man's strength, rendering him in a certain sense like a woman – i.e., physically weak and confined to the indoors. The rabbis thus interpret the word "*ishim*" in the verse "Unto you, O men (*ishim*), I call" – as referring to those who possess the qualities of both men (*anashim*) and women (*nashim*): "Rabbi Berakhiah said: These are the Torah sages, who are like women, but perform the valiant deeds of men" (*Yoma* 71a). Rashi explains the sages' similarity to women in that they are "humble and frail." A Torah sage, the spiritual paragon, thus reflects a composite of female and male qualities. Humility and frailty on the one hand, and intellectualism on the other. The valor to which Rabbi Berakhiah refers lies in fighting the war of Torah, according to talmudic commentator R. Samuel Eliezer ben Judah Levi Edels (*Maharsha*), or in subduing the evil inclination, according to another interpretation. This is reminiscent of the ideas of Carol Gilligan, as expressed in her book *In a Different Voice*.

In fact *haskalah* criticism (Y.L. Gordon, for example) mocked the yeshivah students' lack of virility, and held what it perceived as excessive intellectualism in contempt. Veneration of physical strength is the antithesis of the diaspora archetype, as expressed in the writings of various thinkers, from Berdichevsky to Rabbi Kook.

I will now return to the main focus of this essay: Israeli law, which comprises both religious-halakhic and civil components. The former component clearly defines the roles of men and women, their rights and obligations, and would appear to be a closed system that cannot be contended with, except by replacement with an alternative system. This is not the case however. Jewish law itself recognizes the power of common practice to determine, *inter alia*, monetary relations between marriage partners. Nevertheless, neither common practice nor changing circumstances have brought rabbinical courts to recognize the equal rights of partners to property acquired during the course of their marriage. Only civil courts have adopted the principle of equality between the sexes with regard to monetary relations between partners.

This issue created an uproar, when the Supreme Court ruled in the Bavli case, that even the rabbinical courts must recognize the principle of civil partnership. The problem is often presented as touching upon the ability of *Halakhah* to adapt to secular law, i.e., can a religious court grant legitimacy to the civil principle of equality between marriage partners, based upon halakhic principles. This approach angers the rabbis, perhaps because it presents them as halakhic technicians, charged with the task of finding formal justification for a ruling inspired by a different and foreign value system. Therein lies the root of the problem – the rabbis' sense of alienation from reality, although the religious public is also a part of that reality. In other words, the question is in fact an internal halakhic one: in ruling in accordance with *Halakhah*, can a religious court ignore the prevailing social and cultural reality, among religious as well as secular Jews, whereby marriage partners see all of their property as being jointly owned.

In the public debate that followed the Bavli ruling, a certain rabbinical court judge stated that he fails to see why a woman should have the right to half of the fruits of her husband's labors, earned by the sweat of his brow at the factory or office. Such unwillingness to internalize values of equality and partnership commonly held in religious circles as well, apparently stems from a feeling that these values pose a threat to the traditional family structure, and that rabbinical court judges should therefore strive to afford such values as little legitimacy as possible. It goes without saying that attempts to shore up a family structure, the premises of which have been cancelled by the reality of the majority of society, are doomed to failure.

Indeed the social climate in which the rabbinical courts function, whereby they are constantly on the defensive in relation to the secular public, makes it difficult to expose religious law to reality. Consequently, they have difficulty in distinguishing between apologetics and internal halakhic issues – which they are duty-bound to address.

The same reasoning also applies to another difficult issue, that of women who are denied divorce. The difficulty of finding some solution or other is often discussed. The main difficulty however, lies in the fact that there is no agreement regarding the existence or scope of the problem. An *agunah*, in the classic sense, is a woman whose husband has disappeared and there is no way of ascertaining his death. Similarly, a woman is considered "denied a divorce" when her husband has fled or refuses to obey a decision obligating him to provide her with a bill of divorce. In such cases, all will agree that there is a halakhic problem requiring a solution.

Only rarely however, are husbands compelled to grant a divorce. The problem is not so apparent when the dispute is financial, and the husband demands far-reaching concessions in return for a divorce. Some women give in to such blackmail, and are prepared to pay a heavy price for the husband's consent, as long as they receive the sought-after divorce. The difficulty lies not in the lack of a halakhic solution, but first and foremost in the lack of awareness that a halakhic problem does exist. Thus no significant effort is made to explore the halakhic potential for a solution. The option of compelling a husband to grant a divorce is not employed, and other available sanctions against reluctant husbands are rarely imposed. There is no willingness to even consider more far-reaching solutions, such as the mechanism of annulling marriages.

There can be no denying, however, that the rabbis' actions are rooted in *a priori* ideological premises: first and foremost the desire to preserve the patriarchal structure of the family. It is thus inconceivable to them that a woman might have the power to disengage from her husband simply because he has become repugnant to her, or claiming that reconciliation is not possible, although in so doing the rabbinical court is in fact acting contrary to the religious interest, whereby refusing to grant a divorce may encourage the couple to live in sin. This is a kind of mirror image of secular permissiveness – the more permissive the generation, the tougher and more intransigent the rabbinical court's positions.

It is important to note that the passivity of the rabbinical courts in Israel has increased, due to their lack of dependence on the religious community. There is a distinct lack of effective pressure that can be brought to bear only by the religious community, since the status of rabbinical court judges is guaranteed by secular legislation. Paradoxically, the enactment of general civil marriage could actually bring the religious authorities to address the internal, religious problem, in all its severity.

The civil component faces its own difficulties and dilemmas. It grants legal authority to religious law, yet denies its responsibility for cases in which men are permitted to remarry (without divorce) and women are not, or the fact that only men are required to pay alimony, for example. The wording of the law that grants authority to religious law in these and other cases does not fully reflect the discrimination against women. The law uses the term "spouse," but in reality, under the guise of such wording, enacts discriminatory practices. In determining who is permitted to remarry, the law discriminates against women as a group, in comparison to men as a group. The problem lies not in the rationale behind the cases in which permission to remarry is granted, nor in the symbolic discrimination inherent to the restrictions against bigamy, nor in what is often seen as the apparently intolerable ease with which such permission is granted. The serious dilemma posed is whether, in light of this discrimination, permission to remarry without divorce should be abolished entirely, causing injustice to deserted husbands, or whether such permission should be upheld, while continuing the tireless struggle to find solutions for deserted wives.

Civil law however is not blameless when it comes to creating a social climate that may result in discrimination against women. First, it perpetuates the image of women as weak and requiring protection, in such cases as broken promises of marriage – which are recognized in the woman's favor, but not in the man's – or in determining the legal age for marriage for girls but not for boys – a law that has only recently been amended. Second, one of the biggest problems in terms of social climate is the advantage afforded to women when it comes to alimony for example, or to custody over children. There are a number of possible approaches to this issue. One approach would be to revoke such advantages, in the interest of equality. The legislature has already begun acting in this vein, in its decision that a woman's income from employment or assets must be considered when determining her right to alimony.

The idea behind this was that the principle of equality requires women to contribute to the family's livelihood. It would seem that in the midst of all the rhetoric, the lawmakers forgot that the function of the court is not to act as a moral guide to the running of the ideal family, but rather to serve as a mediator between the partners in their struggle to sever the ties between them, and the conditions under which they will do so. The opposite approach asserts that the advantages enjoyed by women should remain in force, so as not to weaken their bargaining position. According to this approach, there is no point in changing only one aspect of relations between the sexes, without effecting overall change. Canceling the advantages enjoyed by women without doing the same with regard to those enjoyed by men, could have an adverse legal effect on the already inferior status of women.

The other side of the coin however, is that under present circumstances, in which the aforementioned advantages are left in force, civil law continues to promote negative social messages, whereby men bear economic responsibility, while women provide nurturing. Such a division unfortunately creates a comfortable route for men to abdicate responsibility for their children, or at best enables them to reduce their responsibility to a purely financial level. We thus often discover that the conservatism represented by the civil courts is no less powerful than that reflected in the rabbinical courts.

"The King's Daughter is all Dignified Within" (Psalms 45:14): Basing Israeli Women's Status and Rights on Human Dignity[1]

ORIT KAMIR

Human Dignity at the Heart of Israel's Bill of Rights

From a constitutional point of view, the early 1990s mark the beginning of the *kvod ha'adam ve-heruto* era in Israeli legal history. In 1992 and again in 1994, the Knesset, Israel's Parliament, enacted Israel's Basic Law: *kvod ha'adam ve-heruto*, which was widely accepted and embraced as the country's long-awaited Bill of Rights. The Basic Law's title was translated into "human dignity and liberty." In fact, whereas the Hebrew *herut* does indeed indicate liberty, *kvod ha'adam* entails a host of diverse values, best captured by the English terms honor, glory, dignity and respect. In the context of Israeli society and culture, these distinct values connote very different – and clashing – political world-views (most significantly nationalistic Zionist, Jewish orthodox and "leftist" liberal perspectives). Of these values, honor has always been predominant in

---

[1] Warm thanks go to Yair Eldan for his immeasurable help in coping with Talmudic sources, and to Maya Steinitz and Yofi Tirosh for inspiring conversation.

Israeli society and culture, as well as most problematic and unacknowledged. The enactment of Basic Law: *kvod ha'adam ve-heruto* manifests a vague, implicit, attempted compromise between the rivalling worldviews and their supporters. In other words: it constitutionally intertwines honor, Israel's underlying value, with glory and dignity.

Significantly, the Basic Law's official translation into English neglects to mention honor, glory and respect, presenting Israel's Bill of Rights as constituting human dignity at the heart of Israel's constitutional value system. This ideological determination echoes the judicial system's explicit interpretation of the Basic Law, which has, understandably, enraged significant sectors of Israeli society, feeding into their growing alienation from the Supreme Court and "its" Bill of Rights.

I have explored these issues in other publications, including an English one, discussing the implications of the many faces of Israel's *kvod ha'adam*.[2] In this paper I focus on human dignity alone, examining its potential implications for the development of Israeli women's socio-legal status and rights. I observe that, given the status of "equality," "dignity" and other values in Israel's Bill of Rights and constitutional rhetoric, dignity is the single most important value for women to utilize in the promotion of their sociolegal status and rights. Since the exact contents and ideological meanings of dignity are still vague and embryonic, it is crucial for women to explore this new area of law and ideology, learning to conceptualize their needs and voice their demands in the emerging framework of human dignity. Reviewing the roots of dignity in

---

[2] See "Honor and Dignity Cultures: The Case of *kavod* (honor) and *kvod ha-adam* (dignity) in Israeli Society and Law," 2002, in *The Concept of Human Dignity in Human Rights Law*, editors David Kretzmer and Ekhart Klein, Amsterdam: Kluwer. For a presentation, in English, of the Basic Law see David Kretzmer's paper in this edited collection.

traditional Jewish thought, I suggest that contemporary Israeli women cannot turn to this cultural heritage, which links women's dignity with their "modesty" and confinement in traditional, stereotypical roles. In their exploration of dignity, Israeli women must look within and listen to their inner voices practicing the language of their dignity.

Basic Law: Human Dignity and Liberty stipulates that "There shall be no violation of the life, body or dignity of any person as such," and that "All persons are entitled to protection of their life, body and dignity." It thus affords human dignity special status among the many values and rights it addresses explicitly and implicitly. Since the Basic Law's enactment, the Supreme Court has been reiterating that it did little other than officially state and validate the central role human dignity has always played in Israeli society and law. In fact, this statement cannot be supported. The Declaration of Independence does number "liberty" among the many values it mentions, but there is no trace of the concept "human dignity" anywhere in this national "credo." Similarly, no other official document has ever mentioned human dignity. Even the rulings of the Supreme Court include only scant and random references to human dignity, and only since the late 1970s. The (claimed) centrality of human dignity to Israeli culture and law is a new phenomenon, beginning in the 1990s. It is thus time to address the issue, and to imbue as yet unformed concepts with substantial legal and ethical content.

Universal and Specific Aspects of Human Dignity

Human dignity is ascribed in the Basic Law to "any person as such." This assertion stresses the universal and absolute nature of this value, applying it to persons of every creed, race, sex, age, sexual preference or social status. This universal nature of human dignity testifies to basic equality of all people who, as human beings, possess human dignity and are equally entitled to be treated accordingly. We are all ends in our own right rather than means to be exploited by others, and equally deserving of such treatment. Indeed, every person is equally entitled to basic "human" living conditions, self-determination and the opportunity to raise a family as s/he desires. Every person is equally entitled to protection against torture, abuse, expulsion, illegal invasion of her/his privacy and the demolition of her/his home.

Human dignity, however, comprises another, more particular aspect. Safeguarding human dignity includes protecting people against humiliation, degradation, and terrorization. Members of groups with diverse histories might feel degraded, humiliated or terrorized by different circumstances. The relatives of a hanged man – so the saying goes – are particularly sensitive to rope. Thus, associating a Jew with an anti-Semitic stereotype could constitute an affront to her/his dignity, although the very same remark when addressed to another person might give no offence whatsoever. Similarly, addressing a person as an "Uncle Tom," or burning a cross on his or her lawn might pose an exclusive offence to the dignity of an African-American.

From this perspective, human dignity may be better suited to address culturally based sensitivities than equality. Focusing on "common denominators" that may serve as basis for equalizing, the rhetoric of equality risks privileging human features and preferences which are unique to the members of powerful, ruling classes, but presented by them as universal "common denominators." Such privileging entails oversight regarding the unique characteristics of members of minority groups. Through the prism of human dignity, it may be possible to respect and defend culture-specific dignity as well as fundamental human common denominators.

The Status of Women in Israel

Israel's Declaration of Independence announces full sex equality. Accordingly, an impressive series of progressive, egalitarian laws flesh out women's extensive legal rights. Israeli legislation is exemplary and outstandingly progressive in its treatment of numerous areas of women's lives (maternity leave rights, liberal regulations governing artificial insemination, financial support to single mothers and protection against sexual harassment are cases in point). Nevertheless, women in Israeli society have never possessed full equal rights. Most significantly, on several issues the law itself restricts women's right to equality. Thus, for example, the very law that constitutes women's equal legal rights explicitly restricts its own application, exempting the whole area of marriage and divorce. What this means is that Israeli women are not entitled to full equality before the law in their family lives. Every woman in Israel is subject, in this important area, to the precepts of religious law as practiced by the community to which the state law relegates her, and to the authority of that community's religious authority and courts. Thus, every Jewish woman is subject to Jewish religious law, as interpreted by the rabbinical court; every Moslem woman to Islamic law, as determined by the *shari'a* court; every Christian woman to the religious law of her Church – none of which award women a status fully equal to men's.[3]

More typically, discriminatory guidelines and regulations govern some areas, which are not directly regulated by state law. Thus, for example, military regulations discriminate against women by barring them from field units, and thus from advancing through

---

[3] For a comprehensive presentation and discussion, in Hebrew, of women's rights under Israeli law, and an extensive bibliography, see Kamir, *Feminism, Rights and the Law*, 2002, Tel Aviv: Ministry of Defence Press.

the military hierarchy. In Israel, a military career is often a required springboard to managerial positions in business and central roles in local and national politics. Women's prevention from getting ahead within the military limits their opportunities in civilian life as well.

Finally, even where law and regulations do not explicitly discriminate against women, patriarchal prejudices, sexist stereotypes, conservatism and fear of change feed and perpetuate underlying social norms, customs and prevailing practices that deny women equal opportunity. As in every other society, misogynist stereotypes prevail, upholding a glass ceiling and barring women from advancing and expanding to new social and economic realms. Commendable, progressive legislation attempts to preclude such practices, but is very difficult to implement. The family's central role in both Jewish and Palestinian Israeli societies places a particularly heavy burden on women. Both societies respond to the national conflict by encouraging women to bear children, thus saddling them with heavy maternal obligations at the expense of other potential options. Despite strict legislative prohibition of discrimination on the basis of family status, pregnancy and parenthood, such practices are widespread.

As in every society, women in Israel face rape, child sexual abuse, prostitution, trafficking, battery, sexual harassment and stalking. Every form of violence against women is appropriately addressed by Israel's criminal code in great detail and with much good will and determination, but law enforcement is lacking, and other war-related national priorities always prevail. Over the last decade, violence against women has elicited public attention, in particular domestic violence leading to murder. General tension and violence breed increasing domestic murders of women in both Jewish and Palestinian Israeli societies. As yet, no adequate means of prevention have been formulated and implemented.

In conclusion, while bluntly discriminating against women in the realm of family life, Israeli law offers women impressively progressive rights in the workplace and exemplary protection against gender-based violence. Social reality is far less impressive. Despite the still prevalent, misleading equality myth, Israeli women suffer every form of violence and discrimination typical of contemporary patriarchal hierarchies in the western world.

The Potential of "Human Dignity" to the Elevation of Women's Status

Equality has always been the predominant concept in the struggle for women's status and rights in Israel as everywhere else worldwide. Nevertheless, the use of equality entails inherent difficulties. One is the prevalent and dangerous intuitive association between "equal" and "similar." This association has taken root in western culture over millennia of adherence to the Aristotelian definition of equality. According to Aristotle, "equality" means treating those "similarly situated" in a similar fashion. Equality does not, therefore, entail similar treatment of those "differently situated." As Professor Catharine MacKinnon has shown, in patriarchy, women are constructed as paradigmatically "different."[4] Since in patriarchy men are the uncontested, "natural," taken-for-granted standard for everything, and since it is men who control all evaluation and definition, women are perceived and constructed (by men) as inherently "different" (from them). "Different" is viewed as "differently situated" in every way, thus deserving of different treatment. In other words, women's "difference" is associated with "inequality," resulting in their construction as "undeserving of equal treatment." In a patriarchal cultural context, therefore, the conceptual proximity between "equality" and "similarity" creates a

---

[4] Catharine MacKinnon, 1987. "Difference and Dominance," in *Feminism Unmodified*, Cambridge: Harvard University Press.

psychological barrier, precluding the perception of women as fully "equal" and entitled to equal rights and opportunities.[5]

Moreover, approaching the status of women through the concept of equality often makes it difficult to focus on problems that are unique and/or significant to women. Since the accepted standard in our society is the male experience, "equality for women" is understood as granting women the same rights possessed by men. This liberal approach is immensely useful in guaranteeing women's equal pay, but is highly problematic for women demanding maternity leave rights, rape-law reforms, legal prohibition of sexual harassment, increased punishment of sex offenders, or funding for breast cancer research. As long as "equality for women" is widely understood to mean "granting women similar rights to men's," it is inherently difficult to see, understand, and deal with women's unique needs within the discourse of equality.[6]

Politically, these conceptual difficulties are coupled, in Israel, with the discriminatory, overtly patriarchal positions espoused by the Jewish religious and *haredi* parties, who bluntly reject the notion of women's equality and their entitlement to fully equal rights. Any discussion of women's equality is perceived by these circles as challenging the *Halakhah* and the accepted divine world order, therefore an outright provocation threatening the fragile Israeli "status-quo" (between orthodox and non-orthodox Jews). In the Israeli reality, thus, very real political interests and power back up the conceptual difficulty inherent in the notion of equality.

The employment of "human dignity" and "women's dignity" may contribute to the elevation of Israeli women's status and rights

---

[5] MacKinnon suggests a new, alternative, non-Aristotelian conceptualization of equality, which overcomes the similarity problem but has, unfortunately, not yet taken root.

[6] This argument is made by MacKinnon in "Difference and Dominance" and other writings.

where "equality" talk has reached a dead end. Universal protection of dignity may call attention to basic "human" problems suffered by many women, such as poverty, violence and abuse. Additionally, approaching women's lives from the perspective of their dignity as human beings may promote better understanding of their essential and unique hardships and needs. For example, the grave damage caused by sexual violence – as well as by insensitive treatment by law-enforcing agencies – may be more readily explained and understood in the context of human dignity than in the conceptual framework based on equality. Moreover and very significantly, the conceptualization of women's issues in human dignity rhetoric minimizes the political controversy, since, unlike equality, human dignity is considered a consensual value in Israeli politics, accepted and respected by religious and *haredi* Knesset members.

Women's Dignity

It is self-evident why, in the context of universal defense of human dignity, women must be protected against hunger, torture and abuse. The application of human dignity to accommodate treatment of women's unique conditions requires imaginative and innovative conceptualization of a derivative concept, "women's dignity."[7]

Women, as a group, have suffered throughout history from unique forms of repression and humiliation under patriarchy and male domination. Women have been defined from an androcentric

---

[7] I am well aware of the essentialistic trap, and refrain from defining "women's dignity" in an essentialistic manner. Israeli women, of course, consist of sub-groups, which may differ significantly in defining their dignity. This whole important realm is, unfortunately, not within the scope of this basic presentation.

perspective and forced to internalize and embrace these definitions. They have been systematically perceived and constructed as inferior to men, irrational, and incapable of governing their own lives or participating in public life. They have been taught to obey, serve and fulfill secondary roles within domestic, professional and social settings. Their abilities have been trivialized; the tasks assigned to them (particularly domestic tasks) have been marginalized, deemed unprofessional and unworthy of recognition or recompense. Their experiences have been excluded from public discourse, determination of collective goals and allocation of resources. They have been precluded from participating in cultural or political endeavors. They have been defined as "belonging" to male relatives, mostly fathers, brothers or husbands, and have not been recognized as autonomous and responsible for their own fate. In other words, patriarchal society has denied them all sources of power and self-esteem it has granted men, relegating them to the sidelines.

As feminist scholarship has been convincingly showing for decades, patriarchal conceptualization and treatment of female sexuality is a central site of women's repression, discrimination and humiliation. Perceived by men as objects of sexual desire, women have been viewed and treated as sexual beings and sex objects for the use of men. From a male perspective, sexuality has been defined as women's central feature, portraying women as "temptation," "stumbling-blocks," and beings whose very presence elicits sexual responses – among men, that is. Women are of course no more or less sexual than men, and men arouse (or fail to arouse) sexual responses (in women) just as women arouse (or fail to arouse) such responses in men. But since men seized the exclusive prerogative of defining women – as well as themselves – from an entirely male perspective, it is little wonder that they defined themselves as possessing a wide variety of multidimensional characteristics, while defining women as first and foremost sexual.

Moreover, since women's sexuality was perceived by men as incomprehensible, uncontrollable, and even threatening, it was deemed dangerous, negative and requiring male control. Natural phenomena associated with female sexuality, such as menstruation, were defined as "impure," and viewed as "disgusting," and many aspects of women's lives were perceived as sexual – and thus negative and in need of supervision. Women's hair, for example, was seen in many cultures as sexual (apparently because men found it sexually attractive), and women in those cultures were therefore required to cover it, or even remove it entirely. Similarly, women's voices were perceived as being sexual, and were therefore restricted in public and sometimes altogether. Various parts of the female body were defined as "seductive," and women were required to conceal them, thus restricting their movement and forcing them to hide from the public eye. The male leg, for example, was considered a limb used for walking, while the female leg was considered an object of desire. A woman who did not cover her leg in accordance with accepted cultural practices was thus seen as sexually "provocative," "asking" for men's sexual attention, "cheap," and even "to blame" if men responded sexually and assaulted her. It is no wonder, therefore, that women in patriarchal societies have learned to view their sexuality as a source of weakness and shame (while men have learned to treat their own sexuality as a source of power and pride).

Just as the treatment of a Jew in a manner echoing anti-Semitism may be humiliating and an affront to her/his human dignity, the treating of a woman in a manner echoing patriarchal sexism and misogyny may humiliate her and constitute an affront to her human dignity – that is, to her woman's dignity. In other words, women's dignity – human dignity unique to women – requires that women not be treated in a manner that links them to their inferior status within patriarchal ideology. More specifically, treating a woman as a sex object, or as a being of secondary importance, who is irrational, incapable of conducting her own affairs and unable to fully participate in any professional or social activities, could be a violation of her woman's dignity. Human dignity, which includes women's dignity, requires, therefore, that women not be treated in this fashion.

Women's Dignity (*kavod*) in Jewish Culture[8]

Attempting to define the concept of "women's dignity" in an Israeli context, a reasonable starting point would be Jewish tradition and cultural heritage. Indeed, this rich cultural repository provides such lovely aphorisms as "a man should always be mindful of his wife's dignity" (*Bava Metzia* 59a), and "a man should love his wife as himself, and dignify her more than himself" (*Yevamot* 62b). Alongside these pretty sayings, however, one can also find in halakhic literature, a profound and systematic association of "women's dignity (*kavod*)" with the most repressive aspects of patriarchal culture. "Women's dignity (*kavod*)" is perceived as inexorably linked to a woman's duty to serve her husband, lord and master, and to her "modesty" – a term that expresses and perpetuates deep discrimination against women in Jewish patriarchal culture.

The explicit association of "women's dignity (*kavod*)" and "modesty" in traditional Jewish literature, as well as the barring of

---

[8] The relevant Hebrew root, expressing Jewish notions of women's dignity is *k.v.d.* As mentioned above, this root connotes, in addition to dignity, honor, respect and glory. I believe that women's *kavod* in Jewish culture features less "dignity" than "glory," but, due to the limited scope of this presentation, I do not address this point here, and refer to dignity alone, translating any *k.v.d* word into dignity (even where the traditional translation is to honor).

women from public life, is rooted primarily in tremendously popular homilies on the verse "The king's daughter is all dignified/glorious within" (Ps. 45:14). The association of woman's dignity with her obligation to be modest appears explicitly in traditional literature, and is presented as follows: "A woman is obligated to be extremely modest, to keep all of her dignity (*kavod*) within, and to conceal herself from every man in the world, in everything possible"; "Modesty requires that a woman be modest in her home, and not go out except when necessary, and therein lies her dignity, as it is written: 'the king's daughter is all dignified within.' And even when she is at home, she must also conduct herself with modesty, to be fully clothed, that even her hair may not be uncovered, and even in her own room, because the more she conceals herself in the ways of modesty, the more righteous and upright her sons will be."

This approach is closely connected to the belief that a woman who steps outside the home is liable to sin and cause others to sin due to her unbridled sexuality and frivolousness ("every woman who goes out in public is destined to sin" – *Midrash Rabbah*, Gen. 8, 12). By the very fact of her dangerous sexual presence, she will cause men to look at her and lust after her: "A woman must sit at home and refrain from going out into the street, lest she sin herself and cause others to sin, for they will be looking at a married woman" (*Midrash Tanhumah*, *Vayishlah* 5). A woman's modesty, her own good and the public (male) good require therefore, that a woman remain at home, far from the public arena. "A woman should always try to be modest […] and not step beyond the threshold of her home except in cases of great need, for a woman who goes out of doors sins and causes others to sin" (*Reshit Hokhmah*, Sect. 4, Ch. *Derekh Eretz*); "Rabbi Yose said that a woman who conceals herself within the home is worthy of marrying the high priest and having sons who will be high priests, as it is written: 'the king's daughter [is all dignified within]'" (*Midrash Tanhumah, Vayishlah* 6).

A woman's dignity is thus inexorably linked to her modesty, which requires that she "conceal herself from every man in the world, in everything possible." Maimonides, the greatest medieval *halakhic* authority, put it particularly well: "It is a disgrace for a woman to go out all the time, abroad or in the streets, and husbands must prevent their wives from so doing, and should not allow them to go out but once or twice a month, as needed, for there is nothing more becoming a woman than to sit in the corner of her house, as it is written: 'The king's daughter is all dignified within'" (*Hilkhot Ishut* 13, 11. This *halakhah* also appears in *Arba'ah Turim, Even Ha'ezer* 73).

The "dignity" of the "modest" woman who remains at home is explicitly associated with her matrimonial role and duty toward her husband and his family. Rabbis have always stressed women's duty to serve their husbands in the home: "A woman is indentured to her husband to be in his home"; "A woman must be by her husband's side, since this is the essence of marriage" (*Igrot Moshe, Orah Hayim* 158). In his summary of Maimonides' position on the linkage of these matrimonial duties with women's dignity, Meir Shoresh writes:

> There is no unequivocal and total *halakhic* requirement here that a woman remain at home, but rather a directive in the spirit of the biblical verse, whereby a married woman should remain at home and perform her duties there, and in so doing, she will have the same level of dignity as that of a king's daughter. If she does not fulfill her duty-dignity, it is a disgrace for her.[9]

---

[9] Meir Shoresh, 1981. "The King's Daughter is all Dignified Within – Sources, Significance and Applicability," *Shma'atin* vol. 64, 57, 69 (Hebrew). Based on his analysis of the positions of other rabbinical authori-

A woman's duty toward her husband and his family is thus to be at home at all times, in order to serve them; *this duty constitutes her "dignity."* A woman's "dignity" therefore lies in her duty to be at home in the service of her husband and his family.

A woman who does not remain at home does not merely lose her dignity and respectability; the Rabbis openly blame her for any evil that may befall her outdoors. Thus for example, they blame Dinah, Jacob's and Leah's daughter, who did not remain at home, but ventured outside and behaved in an undignified manner, for having caused Shekhem to rape her. *Midrash Tanhumah* explains:

> The Torah alludes to this matter – that a woman should not venture out too much – as it is written: 'And God blessed them [and God said unto them, Be fruitful, and multiply, and replenish the earth,] and subdue it ...' (Gen 1:28). 'And subdue **it**' (*vekhivshuha*) is written like 'And subdue **her**' (*vekhivshah* – without the letter *vav*) – a man subdues a woman, but a woman does not subdue a man. If, however, a woman goes about in public excessively, she will come to sin and harlotry. Such was the case of Dinah, the daughter of Jacob. As long as she remained at home, she did not come to sin, but once she ventured outside, she caused herself to come to sin (*Tanhuma, Vayishlah* 12).

The Rabbis have no qualms about blaming Dinah's mother, Leah, as well: "Since it is written that Leah went out to meet Jacob (Gen 30:16), her daughter was also wont to go out and be a harlot, who brought her rape by Shekhem upon herself."

---

ties, Shoresh concludes that this rationale is not limited to married women: even the dignity of a single woman depends upon her remaining at home. "If in the case of a married woman we stated that her dignity is to serve her husband and family, in the case of a single woman, there is dignity merely in her remaining inside the home," *ibid.* p. 63.

Moreover, women's dignity is derivative of "public dignity," that is the dignity of men. The connection is as follows: the very presence of a woman – just like the sight of her uncovered hair, the sound of her speaking aloud, singing, or chanting the Torah – is perceived in many sources as violations of public dignity, male dignity. (The best-known statement to this effect can be found in the Talmud, *Megilah* 23a: "The Rabbis said: 'A woman may not chant the Torah, for reasons of public dignity'.") "Public dignity" therefore requires that women be excluded from public life. A woman "dignifies" society by her absence from the public arena, conceals herself at home and is thus herself dignified. In other words, a woman's dignity depends upon and derives from the respect she shows for (male dominated) society by staying away from the public domain.

For centuries, countless sages and scholars (all of them men – including the contemporary, academic Meir Shoresh) addressed questions such as the following: Since a woman is not allowed to leave the house, is her husband required to support her financially when she has killed someone by accident and is forced to seek asylum? Is a woman permitted or obligated to leave the house for the sake of fulfilling a religious duty, or in the case of a religiously mandated war? (Many believe that she may not go out even to return a lost item or to attend legal proceedings in which she is involved.) For many centuries, there was a general consensus that a woman's "dignity," "duties" and "modesty" precluded her leaving the house altogether (except perhaps in cases of dire necessity).[10]

_____

[10] Based on four articles he published on this theme, Meir Shoresh concludes that conscription of women should be opposed, since military service jeopardizes women's modesty, and that military service cannot justify any deviation from the rule of "the king's daughter is all dignified

In significant parts of traditional Jewish culture, women's dignity is thus not a basic, human, liberal right. Rather, it is a socio-religious status that expresses and imposes upon women obligations of "modesty" and matrimonial service that bar them from public life and lock them up at home, silencing and subjecting them to their husbands' authority. This type of "women's dignity" compels women to assume patriarchal female roles and images, denying them the right to self-determination. This type of "women's dignity" presumes, expresses and perpetuates humiliating stereotypical images of women's bodies, sexuality, personal abilities and place in the world. This type of "women's dignity" confines women out of consideration for the male community, apparently incapable of tolerating female presence. This type of "women's dignity" is a restrictive and repressive concept.

In seeking content for "women's dignity," suitable to Israeli society and law, these traditional sources cannot provide inspiration. Furthermore, we must beware of the influence repressive patriarchal views might exert – through language – on the contemporary, emerging notion of "women's dignity." To undercut the negative impact of rabbinical interpretation of the verse "The king's daughter is all dignified within," and hoping to free this idiom from the confines of patriarchal culture, I propose a new, alternative interpretation.[11] A fitting meaning of "The king's

within." His positions, expressed in contemporary style, uncritically accept the traditional patriarchal values *in toto*.

[11] To complete the picture, the biblical verse should be read in its full context: "Hearken, O daughter, and consider, and incline thine ear; forget also thine own people, and thy father's house. So shall the king greatly desire thy beauty; for he is thy Lord; and worship thou him. And the daughter of Tyre shall be there with a gift; even the rich among the people shall entreat thy favour. The king's daughter is all dignified/glorious within: her clothing is of wrought gold" (Ps. 45:11–14). Whatever these verses may mean, there is no doubt that their clearly

daughter is all dignified within" is that only the king's daughter herself – not the king, nor any who would curtail and imprison her in a corner of her house – can and may define her own "dignity." This self-determination of the king's daughter will come from "within," and will not be rooted in any extraneous concepts of "public (male) dignity," or images of a king's daughter as conceived through the eyes of men who look at her but see only their own desires, fears and needs. The dignity (and glory) of a queen's daughter is indeed found in her inner self, her experiences, self-perception, desires, fears and the ambition to achieve self-fulfillment. The queen's daughter, the queen and all of their women subjects must set aside extraneous, restrictive and repressive images, and define themselves and their dignity from within.

This reading of the biblical verse expresses the two basic principles that constitute the framework for a contemporary approach to human dignity: the liberal principle, as established by John Stuart Mill, which defines each individual as autonomous, free and entitled to self-determination, and the Kantian categorical imperative, which requires that every person be treated as an end to her/himself and never only as a means to an end.

Israeli law must facilitate and support women's efforts in seeking self-determination, defining women's dignity, and establishing social values worthy of recognition and protection. The legal system must actively participate in this undertaking, and integrate its results into the normative framework of Israeli society.

---

patriarchal context makes them anachronistic and irrelevant to our times. My suggestion of a new reading of verse 14 does not pretend, of course, to reflect the verse's original meaning, but strives to free it from the exegetical baggage it has amassed over the years.

Sexual Harassment as a Violation of Women's Dignity in Israeli Law

I would like to conclude on an optimistic note, with an example of how Israeli law may imbue the concept of "women's dignity" with positive content and look to it to derive women's rights. To do so, I briefly present the position taken by Israeli law on the issue of sexual harassment.

The term "sexual harassment" was popularized in the United States in the 1970s. The narrowest and most basic definition of sexual harassment refers to the unwelcome treatment of a person, usually a woman, as a sex object. (A wider variety of chauvinistic and sexist behavior is commonly defined as sexual harassment today. For reasons of economy, I have chosen to mention only this basic definition.) This type of harassment involves unwelcome behavior relating to a woman's sexuality, which forces her to perceive herself as sexual when she would rather not do so. Consequently, the woman feels invaded and violated, and experiences a sense of weakness, shame and/or apprehension. Sexual harassment denies a woman the right to define herself as she sees fit, as any autonomous rational human being is entitled to; it associates her, against her will, with patriarchal stereotypes of women as sexual in every context and always available for the sexual use of men.

A woman's sexuality can and should be a source of pleasure, power and self-fulfillment for her. Every woman is entitled, of course, to realize her sexuality in any way she sees fit (as long as she does not harm others). A welcome sexual approach of a woman is clearly positive and desirable. But relating to a woman as a sexual being when she is not interested in such an approach, assigns her a certain, familiar place within the context of the patriarchal world view, relegating her to a secondary, inferior, subservient and unequal role. Relating to a woman as a sexual being when she is not interested in such an approach, may be humiliating to her, just as racist behavior toward an African American or anti-Semitic behavior toward a Jew may be humiliating to them. Sexual harassment, therefore, undermines a woman's self-confidence, damages her faith in herself, restricts her ability to choose her own self-image, and decreases her chances of integrating into society as a full human being, endowed with equal rights and opportunities. Sexual harassment thus violates women's dignity.[12]

On March 8th 1998 (International Women's Day) the Knesset approved Israel's new sexual harassment law. The first article of the law states that its goal is "to prohibit sexual harassment, in order to safeguard human dignity, liberty and privacy, and in order to promote equality between the sexes."[13] The explanatory notes accompanying the law pronounce its chosen perspective and social goals, stating *inter alia*, the following:

> In the State of Israel, as in other parts of the world, sexual harassment is a common social phenomenon that harms many people, especially women. Sexual harassment constitutes a violation of human dignity, liberty, privacy and the right to equality. It adversely affects the self-respect and social standing of the har-

---

[12] In American feminist theory and jurisprudence sexual harassment is conceptualized in terms of equality, not human dignity. For previous, comprehensive discussion of these differing points of view, and a full presentation of Israel's sexual harassment law, see "Dignity, Respect and Equality in Sexual Harassment Law: Israel's New Legislation," 2003, forthcoming, editors Catharine MacKinnon and Reva Segal, Yale University Press, and, in Hebrew, "Sexual Harassment: Sex Discrimination, or an Injury to Human Dignity?," 1998, *Mishpatim*, vol. 29, 317-388.

[13] Although the law was intended first and foremost to protect women from sexual harassment, it equally prohibits sexual harassment of men, as well as the humiliation and degradation of homosexuals and lesbians based on their sexual orientation.

assed. It degrades her/his humanity, *inter alia* by treating her/him as a sex object for the harasser's use. Sexual harassment denies the harassed person autonomy and control over her/his body, sexuality and right to self-determination; it invades her/his privacy, and discriminates against her/him. Sexual harassment of women humiliates them with regard to their sex or sexuality and impedes their integration as equals in the workplace and other areas of life, thus compromising their equality.

The new law thus adopts the perception of sexual harassment as a violation of human dignity in general and women's dignity in particular, legally condoning and sanctioning it. By law, each of the following types of conduct is now defined as sexual harassment, therefore as illegal violation of human dignity and women's dignity: sexual blackmail, assault, repeated unwelcome sexual propositions, repeated unwelcome references to a person's sexuality, humiliation or degradation of a person based on her/his sex, gender or sexuality, including sexual orientation.[14]

Israel's new sexual harassment law constitutes an important breakthrough in defense of human dignity in general and women's dignity in particular. It is the first systematic attempt by Israeli law to define "women's dignity," types of conduct that might violate it, and legal means of protecting it. In its pursuit of these goals, the law adopts a woman-centered perspective of women's lives, affording women self-determination and control. Let us hope that such legislation will engender serious public discourse as well as helpful judicial decisions regarding women's dignity in Israel, and that it will be a sign of further legal developments. Many additional legal issues require re-evaluation in light of the developing notion of

---

[14] Additionally, the law provides special protection to those in positions of dependence, subordination or vulnerability due to social hierarchy (such as minors, employees, patients).

women's dignity (and liberty). Foremost among these are family-law issues, such as denial of divorce, ineligibility to marry, levirate marriage, surrogacy and the entire issue of marriage and divorce, as well as other women-related issues, including pornography, prostitution and abortion. Time is pressing and work is plentiful, as the Jewish saying goes.

Israeli Divorce Law:
The Maldistribution of Power, its Abuses,
and the "Status" of Jewish Women

SUSAN WEISS

A number of years ago, while working as a divorce lawyer, the rabbinical court ordered my client's husband to grant her a divorce. Such a ruling was, and still remains, difficult to obtain. Rabbinical courts hesitate to issue such orders, preferring to encourage the parties to reach an agreement between them (for reasons I will explain below). It was an important ruling, until the Supreme Rabbinical Court reversed it.

The Supreme Rabbinical Court wrote:

> There would appear to be some justice in the husband's claim that he should not be ordered [to grant his wife a divorce] based on the wife's complaint that he has been unfaithful, since […] he has not been warned, as the *Hakham Zvi* has written […]. Furthermore […] even a husband who beats his wife, with regard to whom the *RaM"A* wrote in ch. 154 art. 3 [of the *Shulkhan Arukh* – tr.] that there are those who say he can be compelled to divorce [his wife] – that is only after he has been warned once or twice […]. However, since the parties have been separated for a long time, a divorce by agreement would be most desirable.

Appalled, and sure that this decision violated the basic human rights of my client, I sent the decision to Attorney Neta Ziv, legal adviser to the Association for Civil Rights in Israel (ACRI). I thought that her office might be willing to file a petition on behalf of my client to the Supreme Court of the State of Israel, sitting in its capacity as the High Court of Justice. Ms. Ziv sympathized with my disappointment at the ruling, but stated unequivocally that nothing could be done about it. She declared: "In Israel, women have the right to be fighter pilots, but they don't have the basic right to get divorced."

By Law: Israeli Women are Not Equal to Israeli Men

I have no doubt that the sources of repression and discrimination against women run deeper than The Law.[1] Israeli women may have the right to be fighter pilots, but, in fact, only one woman has exercised this right since the IDF changed its policies. Laws on the books are insufficient in and of themselves to effect great social reform. Yet few modern, liberal, democratic countries at the turn of the millennium have laws that openly and clearly affirm the inequality between women and men. Israel is one of them. In matters of marriage and divorce, Israeli law explicitly maintains that women are not equal to men.

On November 2, 1991, Israel ratified the "Convention on the Elimination of all Forms of Discrimination against Women"

---

[1] J. Donovan, 1988. "Enlightened Liberal Feminism," *Feminist Theory*, p. 30: "Liberalism is limited in that while it may provide justice for means, it does not afford morality of ends"; C.A. Mackinnon, "Not by Law Alone: From a Debate with Phyllis Schafly," *Feminism Unmodified*, pp. 21, 26: "The law alone cannot change our social condition. It can only help. So far, it has helped remarkably little."

(CEDAW). Article 16 requires all signatory countries to take every measure to eliminate discrimination against women in all matters pertaining to marriage, family relations and divorce. At the end of the treaty, Israel entered the following reservation:

> The State of Israel hereby expresses its reservation with regard to Article 16 of the Convention, insofar as the laws of personal status binding on the several religious communities in Israel do not conform with the provisions of that Article.

Israel's reservation to CEDAW mirrors a similar reservation set forth in article 5 of the "Equal Rights for Women Law – 5710–1951." There too Israeli law stipulates "there shall be one law for women and men alike," except with respect to "religious laws pertaining to marriage and divorce." When the Ministry of Justice attempted in 1992 to initiate legislation of a new "Basic Law" entitled "Basic Human Rights" that included a similar reservation, the women's organizations objected, refusing to perpetuate the inequality of women by legal fiat and official legislation.

By Law: The Personal Status of Married Women in Israel Is Determined by the (Almost) Unfettered Discretion of Their Husbands (and Not by the State). Women Have No Right to Divorce Except with the Consent of Their Husbands.

Israeli law sanctions the "inequality" of women in the area of marriage and divorce in order to make room for the "Rabbinical Courts Jurisdiction (Marriage and Divorce) Law – 5713–1953" that gives the rabbinical courts exclusive jurisdiction over marriage and divorce of "Jews in Israel, being nationals or residents of the State." The rabbinical courts rule in accordance with Jewish law *(halakhah).* Jewish law does not give women and men equal status upon the dissolution of the marriage.

The rabbinical court judges recognize the authority of biblical law, and hold that a marriage is over only when a husband gives his wife a writ of divorce (a *get*), [2] of his own free and unfettered will.[3] They do not recognize the authority of the state to intervene between the parties and declare a marriage over. They do not acknowledge a woman's right to give her husband a bill of divorce. And, not wanting to infringe upon the husband's free will, they hesitate to wield whatever power and authority they do have under Jewish law to compel, order or even just persuade a husband to grant his wife a divorce.[4] And when the courts do take the initiative and finally exercise their authority to order the husband to give his wife a *get*, the injunction is often insipid and unenforceable. If a husband remains recalcitrant, is missing, mentally incompetent, unconscious, or indifferent to pressure that would sway a reasonable man, his wife remains married to him until he is convinced, found, or regains his faculties or consciousness for long enough to give his wife a bill of divorce.

---

[2] Deut. 24:1 "When a man hath taken a wife, and married her, and it come to pass that she find no favor in his eyes, because he hath found some uncleanness in her: then let him write her a bill of divorcement, and give it in her hand, and send her out of his house."

[3] Mishnah, Yevamot 112b: "A man who divorces is unlike a woman who divorces, for a woman is divorced willingly or unwillingly, and a man divorces only of his own volition."

[4] See the rabbinical courts' report on "The Jurisdiction of Rabbinical Courts Law (Enforcement of Rulings to Compel Divorce, Exigent Measure 5755–1995)." The report notes that in the Central District, legal sanctions to compel husbands to grant a divorce were imposed only twice during the period 1996–1.1.98.

In the State of Israel, it is the husband who determines the personal status of his wife – whether she is married or divorced. In other words, in Israel, a woman's right to divorce and remarry is subject to the discretion of her husband.

On the other hand, a husband's right to divorce and remarry does not hinge upon the good will of his wife. The State of Israel and the rabbinical courts will intervene on a husband's behalf in order to safeguard his right to end a failed marriage, and to ensure his right to enter into a new marriage and conjugal relationship. While it is true that the rabbinical courts abide by the amendment of Rabbi Gershom *Me'or Hagolah*, whereby a woman cannot be divorced against her will,[5] this amendment is merely a rabbinical edict, and not biblical law. The courts can bypass rabbinical amendments and fetter, curtail or circumscribe the free will of a woman if it feels that it is necessary to do so in the interest of justice. If a woman refuses to accept a *get* from her husband because she is recalcitrant, missing, insane, in a coma or indifferent to pressures that might otherwise move a reasonable woman, the rabbinical courts have a solution. The rabbis can authorize a husband to take a second wife – an extreme action that the rabbis may very well take if, for example, the wife has committed adultery and refuses to accept a writ of divorce; or if she has abandoned her husband's home and cannot be found to accept the *get*. Article 179 of the Penal Law – 5737–1977 recognizes such court orders as legitimate exceptions to the law prohibiting polygamy. The principles of reason, morality, The Law and the rabbinical courts' sense of justice will all intervene and maneuver to protect a man's rights to marry and divorce.

A husband's personal status, as opposed to that of his wife, is not determined by his spouse. It is determined and protected by a higher authority.

---

[5] See Z. Falk, 1966. *Jewish Matrimonial Laws in the Middle Ages*, pp. 13–18.

The Inequality Between Women and Men with Regard to Divorce and the Resulting Maldistribution of Power Causes Injustices of Various Kinds:

The Law Condones the Blackmail of Women:

When faced with a recalcitrant husband, the rabbinical courts, hesitant by conviction, often deflect cases rather than decide them. They prefer to secure a husband's resolute agreement to give his wife a divorce, rather than to rule that he must grant a divorce and impose sanctions until he agrees to do so. They want to avoid issuing decisions that the husband may ignore (or worse, may infringe on his free will). Instead, the rabbinical court judges prefer to encourage, persuade, cajole and entice a husband to cooperate. If the price is right, many husbands can be persuaded to willingly divorce their wives.

Similarly many women, eager to procure their husbands' willing agreement to grant them a divorce before they are too old or too gray or too exhausted, can be persuaded to pay the suggested price. In exchange for the *get*, they will waive their rights to child-support, joint property, and sometimes even the custody of their children. Women may pay hundreds of thousands of shekels in return for the privilege to divorce. (The price is usually in inverse proportion to the integrity of the husband and his attorney.) The courts – both civil and rabbinical – do not interfere in this process of exchange, and do not try to redistribute the imbalance of power and authority given to the husband.

In fact, the religious authorities condone payment in return for a divorce, and even encourage it, as a valid, efficient and religiously acceptable method of divorce resolution. Blackmail does not invalidate a Jewish divorce.[6]

In a similar vein, the Supreme Court has upheld the validity of contracts in which women have waived their various property and legal interests in return for a writ of divorce, refusing to find that such divorce agreements were signed under duress. The civil court has deemed a *get* sufficient "consideration" in exchange for the relinquishing of those interests.[7] Justice Haim Cohn wrote: "A divorce agreement is no different from any other kind of agreement. One who wishes to obtain something, gives up that which is rightfully his, or offers additional payment, in order to secure the object of his desire."[8]

The legal system has embraced this arrangement of payment in return for a *get* as an efficient and legitimate solution to the plight of Jewish women seeking divorce – even when the husband is to blame for the break-up of the marriage, and even when the agreement compromises the children's rights to child-support. If a woman pays for her divorce, Israeli courts will rise to the defiance of free enterprise and "the best interests of the principles of contract"[9] and approve the agreement.

---

[6] Rabbi H.S. Sha'anan, 5750, "Ways of Coercing Divorce," 11 *Tehumin* 203 (5750).

[7] See for example, C.A. 573/82 Barak v. Barak 38 (4) 626, 633 (1985). ("The wife was clearly eager to receive a divorce and be released from her husband's bonds. In order to attain this goal, she was prepared to make far-reaching material concessions. The agreement should not however be seen as lacking return, just as one should not determine, based solely on its terms, that the wife had been exploited.")

[8] C.A. 162/72 Amzalag v. Amzalag P.D. 27 (1) 582, 587.

[9] See F.H. 4/82 Cott v. Cott P.D. 38 (3) 197. Justice Aaron Barak uses the term "good of the contract" when determining the validity of indemnity clauses intended to prevent future claims by the mother to increase

The Law Condones the Abuse of Women:

Blackmail is a recognizable and definable form of abuse, but it is only a matter of money. The fact that the law does not allow women to dissolve difficult marriages without the consent of their abusive husbands, fosters both physical and emotional violence. Such law implies that abuse of women is a tolerable phenomenon, in accordance with the rules of society, and promulgated by its judges. If the law condones the abuse of women when they seek assistance from the courts, abuse inflicted far from the public eye must certainly be tolerable.[10]

Susan Moller Okin, in her book, *Justice, Gender and the Family*, claims that the imbalance of power in married life in the husband's favor (including, for example, the power to dissolve the marriage), and the accompanying detriment to the wife, are the causes of abuse. She writes: "There is no doubt that family violence, as it affects both wives and children, is closely connected with differentials of power and dependency between the sexes."[11] "…The basis for wife-beating is male dominance – not superior strength or violent temperament … but social, economic, political, and psychological power."[12]

---

child-support beyond the sum appearing in the divorce agreement. Justice Barak sought to reconcile the "good of the contract" with the "good of the minor." *Cf.* the ruling issued by Justice Shohat in case no. 065190/98 (5740, Tel-Aviv) (indemnity agreements are invalid).

[10] Some scholars claim that *Halakhah* itself encourages abuse of women by turning its back on battered women. See e.g., B. Horsburgh, 1995, *Lifting the Veil of Secrecy, Domestic Violence in the Jewish Community*, 18 Harv. L. J. 171.

[11] S.M. Okin, 1989. *Justice, Gender and the Family*, p. 129.

[12] *Ibid.* p. 152, quoting Linda Gordon.

It is a sad but well-known fact that many women in Israel are battered by their husbands. The Israel Women's Network (IWN) estimates that one in seven married women is a victim of spouse abuse. In the first 7 months of 1999, seven women were killed in Israel by their husbands, and a much higher number of victims of physical and emotional abuse was reported.

Studies show that Jewish women avoid initiating divorce proceedings and remain within failed marriages for many more years than non-Jewish women.[13] It is reasonable to assume that Jewish women avoid suing for divorce since the dissolution of their marriage lies in the hands of their husbands, and since women's pleas before the courts for interference and help all too often fall on deaf ears. Moreover, it is possible that they may fear a drop in their standard of living, even to the point of destitution. The price of divorce is simply too high.

Civil Law Does Not Safeguard the Property of Women:

Israeli family law denies women full access to property accrued during the course of marriage: According to the "Spouses (Property Relations) Law – 5733–1974," women are theoretically entitled to half the value of all property accrued during the course of marriage. But according to article 5 of the law, this right accrues only upon the "dissolution of the marriage." When a husband refuses to grant his wife a divorce, there is no "dissolution of the marriage," and the wife therefore has no cause of action upon

---

[13] See *http://www.JewishWomen.org/domestic.htm*

which to base her claim to property accrued during the course of the marriage.[14]

Thus, just as the "Rabbinical Courts Jurisdiction (Marriage and Divorce) Law – 5713–1953" makes a woman's right to divorce contingent upon the agreement and good will of her husband, so too the Spouses (Property Relations) Law makes a woman's rights to property accrued during the course of marriage contingent upon that same agreement and good will. According to the laws of the State of Israel, an Israeli Jewish husband holds the power to determine whether his wife is married or not. And he has the same power, by law, to decide how much marital property his wife is entitled to, if any.

In the Ya'akobi-Knobler ruling, former Chief Justice Meir Shamgar referred to the Spouses (Property Relations) Law as a "dead letter" law. And, in the attempt to dismiss the Spouses Property Relations law in favor of an alternative arrangement that would allow women to claim their share of family property before the dissolution of marriage, Chief Justice Shamgar argued that "it was obviously not the legislator's intention [regarding the Spouses Property Relations Law] to create an arrangement … that not only fails to afford equal treatment [to both parties], but actually increases the advantage of the stronger party."[15]

---

[14] See C.A. 1915/91, 2084/91, 3208/91 Ya'akobi v. Ya'akobi, Knobler v. Knobler P.D. 49 (3) 529 (1995), in which five judges presented four different approaches to this law. It should also be noted that the Financial Relations Law applies to couples married from 1.1.74. If married before this date, the wife has the right to claim that she is a partner in assets accrued during the course of marriage, according to the "joint possession" arrangement. This arrangement does not guarantee that a woman will be able to obtain half of the property accrued during marriage either. This subject is, however, beyond the scope of this article.

[15] P.D. 49 (3) 529, 569.

Time after time, former Chief Justice Shamgar described how the Spouses (Property Relations) Law stands in direct opposition to the principles of equality between the sexes and social justice that should, in his opinion, serve the entire legal system as a guide and reflect modern values and sensibilities. The Spouses (Property Relations) Law purports to guarantee both partners equal property rights, when in fact it "violates" the rights of one side, while affording "unfair advantage" to the other. It gives one of the partners the opportunity to take advantage of the marital property arrangements, impose his will upon the other partner, and force her to accept his conditions. Justice Shamgar wrote: "[This is] a property arrangement with outrageous and absurd consequences, which grants one of the parties license to cynically manipulate and abuse the judicial process."[16]

The Injustice to Women Does Not Stem from the Spirit of *Halakhah*, but from its Arbiters

Halakhah is not a collection of harsh and uniform rules, but rather embraces various and contradictory voices. The outcome of a given legal case depends upon the rabbinical authority consulted, the "facts" he deems worthy of emphasis, and the voices he chooses to heed.

Indeed, the rabbinical courts in Israel interpret and apply *halakhah* in a fashion that affords the husband nearly exclusive control over the personal status of his wife; and, as such, may well reject her petition for divorce until her husband has first been warned not to beat her, or not to have an affair with another woman, as did the appeals rabbinical tribunal described at the beginning of this article. Such decisions, however, stem from a

---

[16] *Ibid.* 550.

predisposition to adhere to those voices within the *halakhah* that emphasize a husband's sovereignty over his wife, and treat a woman as her husband's acquisition or property,[17] rather than his partner. Property has no voice of its own, no desires, no feelings and no requests.

There are, however, other voices in *halakhah* that treat wives as partners, not property. These sources listen to women's voices and demands. One such authority is Maimonides, who ruled that if a woman loathes her husband, he is forced to divorce her – "for she is not like a captive, who must lie with someone whom she despises."[18] Maimonides asks the rabbinical judges to internalize a woman's suffering and feelings – like the regional rabbinical court that indeed ordered the abusive and unfaithful husband to divorce his wife.

And there are those rabbinic scholars, educators, and leaders who have found in *halakhah* values and principles that promote equality between women and their partners, and who strive to put an end to the abuse of women by their husbands in the name of *halakhah*.

Bar-Ilan University Rector Rabbi Emmanuel Rackman claims that there are many cases in which *halakhah* permits the rabbis to declare a marriage null and void, thereby precluding any need for the husband to deliver a writ of divorce to his wife as a condition

---

[17] See e.g., J.D. Bleich, "Kiddushei Ta'ut: Annulment as a Solution to the Agunah Problem," *Tradition* 33 (1), p. 114, note: "The legalistic essence of marriage is, in effect, an exclusive conjugal servitude conveyed by the bride to the groom [...] Understanding that the essence of marriage lies in the conveyance of a 'property' interest by the bride to the groom serves to explain why it is that only the husband can dissolve the marriage."

[18] Maimonides, *Hilkhot Ishut*, 14, 8.

for the dissolution of the marriage. Rabbi Rackman has even established a rabbinical court to issue such rulings.

Meir Simcha Feldblum, professor of Talmud at Bar-Ilan University, has examined "different types of associations between men and women in the [traditional] sources, and the manner in which women may end such associations." Feldblum proposes changing the Jewish marriage ceremony to resemble an alternative type of association he refers to as *"derekh hakidushin."* According to Professor Feldblum: "This type of marriage will prevent the creation of *agunot* (anchored wives), consequently reducing the number of *mamzerim* (offspring of adulterous relations) in Israel, as well." In a marriage founded on *derekh hakidushin*, no writ of divorce would be required of the husband should the wife wish to dissolve the association.[19]

It is those persons who interpret and apply *halakhah*, and not *halakhah* itself, who are responsible for the injustice occasioned by today's special circumstances. If we blame "the rules," rather than those who apply them, we absolve them and ourselves of moral responsibility. Women will suffer, and their husbands will humiliate, degrade, revile, beat, abuse, oppress and take unfair advantage of them; husbands will trap their wives in failing marriages; women will be forced to pay for their freedom, and will be denied full access to property accrued during the course of marriage. And no one will be held accountable, since everything is "the responsibility of *halakhah*."

It is clear that blame does not lie with God. He is not guilty of the injustice suffered by women. God gave man the right and responsibility to interpret and enforce His laws, as it is written, "It

---

[19] M.S. Feldblum, 5757–8. "The Problem of *Agunot* and *Mamzerim* – Proposal for a Comprehensive Solution (Proposal for Halakhic and Ideological Discussion)," *Dinei Yisrael* 19:203–216.

is not in heaven."[20] *Halakhah*, as the term itself implies (deriving from the root HL"Kh, meaning: to walk, move, progress – tr.), like other legal systems,[21] is a living, breathing organism, and as such is flexible and in keeping with the injunction: "And you shall live by them." *Halakhah* should not stagnate, while social reality changes and demands new and different responses.

The injustice suffered by women must compel our leaders to overcome their hesitancy to propose and apply creative solutions from within *halakhah*. They must confront the challenge of moral responsibility.

If Those Who Are in Charge of Applying *Halakhah* Continue to Interpret It in the Same Conservative Fashion, Israeli Society Will Have to Bear Moral Responsibility and Take Action.

If the rabbis insist on the limited scope of *halakhah*, and fail to find a *halakhic* solution to the injustice suffered by women, secular society will no longer be able to remain silent and absolve itself of responsibility for this suffering. Israeli society, and especially legislators and judges, must take steps to rectify the injustice caused by those charged with interpreting *halakhah*.

Our judges have a great deal of authority and latitude to exercise discretion in applying the law. Family Court judges should adopt the positions espoused by Justices Shamgar and Dorner, or by Justice Strasberg-Cohen, in the Ya'akobi-Knobler ruling, in

---

[20] Eruvin 55a.

[21] J. Frank, "The constant development of unprecedented problems requires a legal system capable of fluidity and pliancy," *Law and the Modern Mind*: 6 (1932).

addressing matters of family property.[22] They should require full disclosure of property by both sides, and fine those who try to conceal assets or otherwise evade full and honest disclosure. I ask the judges to interpret the term "property" in a creative fashion, expanding the definition with regard to the balancing of marital property to include, for example: good will, professional license, and earning potential (personal capital).[23] They should treat a husband's refusal to grant a divorce as an act that is not in "*in good faith*," thus abrogating his right to seek aid and relief from the courts in ancillary matters relating to the divorce. Similarly, they should invalidate divorce agreements that were signed under duress and that compromise the wife's rights in exchange for a writ of divorce from the husband.

It is incumbent upon Israeli society to amend the Spouses (Property Relations) Law in such a manner that will enable our judges to award a woman half of the property accrued during the course of marriage even before the official dissolution of a marriage through the granting of a writ of divorce (taking care to deny similar relief to a husband who denies his wife a *get*). Israeli society should enact laws that would facilitate the payment of compensation (a form of 'alimony') to a woman by her husband even after divorce in the case of long-time marriages. We should charge lawyers involved in divorce agreements entailing blackmail or deception, with a breach of ethics, or even criminal behavior. And we should demand that husbands who deny their wives a Jewish divorce pay damages to their wives for the pain, suffering, and

---

[22] See above, n. 14.

[23] See "The Financial Relations between Partners Law – Assessment on behalf of IWN," 26.4.98 (unpublished).

losses incurred.[24] **Israeli society, which continues to remain silent in the face of injustice inflicted upon women in the name of *halakhah*, also bears responsibility for the resulting injustice.**

The Law Is a Reflection of Society, Its Values, and Its Power Structures

In enabling the oppression of women by law, a society reflects its values and the power groups at work within it. In Israeli society we claim that women are equal to men, and hence full partners in marriage as well. Yet, as long as the law, its makers, interpreters and enforcers fail to support this equality – the assertion remains little more than lip service.

We must recognize and understand that The Law is not always just, but sometimes inflicts harm and causes damage. A society must examine its laws, lawmakers, interpreters and enforcers, in order to ascertain its goals, whether they are being achieved, and in what fashion. The Law is a powerful tool – for good and for bad.

---

[24] See in File No. 39500/00 Jerusalem Family Court, Doe v. Doe (Judge Greenberger) (23/1/2001) and Motion No. 054233/01 in File No. 9101/00, Doe v. Doe (Judge Marcus) (3/2/2002) (both judges denied husbands' motions to dismiss for lack of cause of action and held that *get* recalcitrance is a tortious act).

We must learn how to use it to mend the world, rather than contributing to its continuous corruption.

It is difficult to examine The Law. The authority and sanction that society affords The Law enables it to conceal its crimes and injustices for years. A *status quo* situation offers security, stability and a sense of order; all change is intimidating. There is little choice however. We must take responsibility and act.

Women's Suffrage: A Halakhic Perspective

DEBORAH WEISSMAN

The issue of the right of women to vote and be elected to office is one of the central sub-chapters of the subject "gender, religion and democracy." In the present context I would like to explore the debate concerning the halakhic aspects of women's suffrage. This is not an original study, but rather a summary of material published elsewhere by important scholars. The three main sources I have employed are:

1. Prof. M. Friedman's book, *Society and Religion*, Yad Ben Zvi, Jerusalem, 1978 (Hebrew).
2. Dr. Y. Cohen, "The Debate between Rabbis Kook and Uziel Concerning Women's Suffrage," *Women in Jewish Sources, Hagut: Compendium of Jewish Thought*, Ministry of Education and Culture, Department for Torah Culture, 1983, pp. 83–95 (Hebrew).
3. Lectures given by Dr. T. Ross in Jerusalem in the 1980s.

I am grateful to these scholars, through whom I was introduced to the fascinating responses of Rabbi Kook and Rabbi Uziel. Before examining the responses themselves however, a few comments on the debate's historical background.

The period in question is that of the *Yishuv* in Palestine under the British Mandate, and the elections for the *Yishuv* institutions: an elected assembly and a national council. At precisely the same time the issue of women's suffrage arose in Palestine, it also arose in western countries such as the United States and England. Even in France – purportedly the cradle of progress – women won the right to vote only in 1944. In this sense, the *Yishuv* kept pace with the democratic west.[1]

The secular Zionist parties advocated formal equality for women, while the *haredi* non-Zionists and anti-Zionists – women and men alike – did not participate in the elections. It was thus only the religious Zionists who were concerned with the issue's halakhic aspect. Naturally, one of the halakhic authorities approached was Rabbi Avraham Yitzhak HaKohen Kook.

---

[1] I would like to dedicate this article to the memory of my father, Dr. Nahum Weissman. A story is told in our family about a conversation between my father and his PhD advisor in the 1930s. My father was a student of history at the University of Paris. He proposed as a topic for his dissertation, something that interested him a great deal at the time: the struggle of women to attain suffrage in western countries. My father wished to explore the topic and its effect on European politics. His advisor however, claimed it was an unimportant and uninteresting subject! He proposed instead, since my father had been born in Turkey, that he research the military history of that country, and more specifically that of a certain 17th century group called the Janissaries. Obedient student that he was, my father indeed wrote his dissertation on that "fascinating" topic. To this day, I doubt whether anyone, other than the advisor himself, has ever read it. I am convinced, on the other hand, that had he pursued the original topic he had chosen, it would have been a pioneer work on a subject of great importance, and who knows where it might have taken him (or us)? Perhaps this story can serve to illustrate the fact that it is not always a good thing for a student to listen to her/his teacher!

Rabbi Kook was born in Latvia in 1865, and immigrated to Palestine in 1904. After serving as Chief Rabbi of Jaffa, he was appointed, in 1921, the first Ashkenazi Chief Rabbi of Palestine – a post he held until his death in 1935. His affinity toward Zionist circles, including the secular Zionists was well-known, although formally not a member of the Zionist movement, not even the religious-Zionist Mizrahi.

Rabbi Kook's response was published in *Nisan* 5680 (1920) in his book *Igrot HaRAYa"H*, and opposed granting women the vote. Before addressing his arguments, I would like to state, for those who are not yet familiar with Rabbi Kook's philosophy, that it would be a mistake to judge one of the greatest Jewish thinkers of the 20th century solely based upon his views on equality for women. To do so would be to dismiss an original, creative and fascinating thinker who has a great deal to contribute to the religious-spiritual experience of the modern Jew. On this particular issue, Rabbi Kook takes a conservative (some would say "reactionary") position. This is not necessarily the case however, with regard to other issues. In any event, his writings and thought are worthy of far greater attention than they receive at present.

Rabbi Kook writes in his response: "I must say that the rabbis who have spoken of the halakhic prohibition thus far have drawn upon the **single voice** (emphasis mine – DW) arising from the Torah, the Prophets and the Writings, from the *Halakhah* and the Midrash, indicating that the spirit of the entire nation, its nature and purity, all stand against this modern innovation." Jewish tradition, as we know, is a culture of debate. It is hard to conceive of other subjects on which there is such consensus in Jewish sources.

The status of women is in fact the subject of numerous debates. For example, the debate in the Mishnah (Sotah) between Ben Azai – who maintains that "one is obligated to teach one's daughter Torah" – and Rabbi Eliezer, who claims that "one who teaches his daughter Torah, it is as if he has taught her foolishness." Another example dates from the Middle Ages. Rabbi Isaac Abrabanel wrote that only men were created in God's image, for only they possess the ability to grasp "the mysteries of creation." Abrabanel's son on the other hand, wrote a philosophical discourse in which one of the participants is a woman, and his contemporary, Rabbi Isaac Arama – author of *Akeidat Yitzhak* – went so far as to write that women, like men "are capable of understanding and accomplishment in matters of wisdom and piety." The reasons for rejecting women's suffrage, according to Rabbi Kook, stem mainly from his concern for modesty and the family. For a more in-depth discussion of the subject, I would refer readers to an article by Yoske Ahituv (a member of the Religious Kibbutz Movement), "Modesty – From Myth to Ethos."[2]

Rabbi Kook wrote: "We believe our perspective on social life to be generally more refined and more pure than that of currently civilized peoples. The family is far more profoundly sacred to us than it is in the entire modern world. And this is the foundation of the happiness and dignity of Jewish women." We thus discover that other peoples must speak in terms of women's rights because their basic condition is degraded. For Jews however, the situation is different. "The rights of Jewish women are based upon the refined content of spiritual worth." Participation in public life and the political arena are thus liable to corrupt this refinement, characteristic of Jewish women, and so undermine the foundations of the family. For this reason, women's suffrage poses a threat to the continuity of Jewish tradition.

According to this approach, denying women the right to vote does not deny them the right to independent opinions. Rabbi

_____

[2] In N. Ilan (ed.), 1999. *Ayin Tovah – Jubilee Volume in Honour of Tovah Ilan*, Hakibbutz Hame'uhad and Ne'emanei Torah Va'avodah, Tel-Aviv (Hebrew).

Kook writes: "We are always prepared to declare the fact that there is a moral duty to listen to the opinions of women in every Jewish home, on general social and political issues as well." Husband and wife must reach an agreement however, and the husband – as the family's "foreign minister" (this term appears in many places, not necessarily in the writings of Rabbi Kook) – is charged with bringing this joint position to the public arena. Rabbi Kook sees this task as a duty rather than a privilege: "The shared opinion must leave the home and the integrity of the family, and the one obligated to bring it to the public domain is the *pater familias*, who is charged with proclaiming the family opinion."

It is important to note that members of the Mizrahi movement, particularly those who lived outside the *Yishuv* at the time, were very disappointed with this response. Pressure was brought to bear on Rabbi Kook to change his position, and in 1926 he agreed to an arrangement of "kosher polling booths," i.e., separate booths for men and women.

Let us now turn to a different response, that of Rabbi Uziel. Rabbi Ben-Zion Meir Hai Uziel was born in Jerusalem in 1880, to a Sephardi family. His more liberal approach was also reflected in his rulings on conversion and abortion. Generally speaking, it is worthwhile examining the positions taken by Sephardi rabbis vis-à-vis modernity, as Prof. Zvi Zohar of Bar Ilan University and the Hartman Institute, and Mr. David Biton – a teacher from Yeruham – have done. Prof. Zohar, Mr. Biton and others have written about figures such as Rabbi Uziel, Rabbi Mashash, and even Rabbi Ovadiah Yosef – at least at the beginning of his career – as being far more "progressive" than their Ashkenazi colleagues. Rabbi Uziel was appointed Chief Sephardi Rabbi of Palestine in 1939, a post he held – later becoming the first Chief Sephardi Rabbi of the State of Israel – until his death in 1953.

Rabbi Uziel's response, published in *Mishpetei Uziel*, was written in 1940, and is preceded by the following comment: "This response was originally written as a personal halakhic inquiry, which I did not wish to publish as a practical ruling." Rabbi Uziel probably did so out of respect for Rabbi Kook, who was his teacher, and later his colleague. He goes on to say however: "Now that this question has been resolved of its own accord, I have decided to publish my response for the greater glory of the Torah." How the question was "resolved of its own accord" we will see toward the end of the article. In the meantime, let us examine Rabbi Uziel's arguments in favor of allowing women to vote. The beginning of the discussion might be a little confusing. Rabbi Uziel distinguishes between "the active choice to vote" and "the passive choice to be voted for." He is of course right grammatically, but we would consider being a candidate (or "running for office") to be far more active than voting. Nevertheless, he writes: "Regarding the former [voting], we have found no clear basis to forbid it, and to deny women this personal right would be untenable." He goes on to present what is in effect a definition of the democratic process: "For in these elections, we appoint our leaders and authorize our elected officials to speak on our behalf, arrange the affairs of the *Yishuv*, impose taxes on our property. Women – directly or indirectly – accept the authority of these officials, obey their public and national directives and laws. How can we have it both ways: imposing upon them the duty to obey the people's elected officials, while denying them the right to elect them?" This is reminiscent of the rallying cry of the American Revolution – "No taxation without representation!"

In the following paragraphs, Rabbi Uziel contends with a series of possible arguments in favor of prohibiting women's suffrage, beginning with the famous rabbinical adage "women are frivolous." "If this is a reason to forbid them to vote," he claims, "then let us also exclude frivolous men, who will never be in short supply." To this he adds the following remark: "Reality would seem to show otherwise – that in the present as in the past, edu-

75

cated and intelligent women are no different from men when it comes to negotiating, buying and selling, and generally conducting their affairs in the best possible fashion." At this point Rabbi Uziel interjects a purely halakhic argument: "Where have we heard of such a thing – appointing a guardian for a grown woman, without her consent?" And if the objection to giving women the vote is – like part of Rabbi Kook's argument – for reasons of modesty, then, Rabbi Uziel replies: "What promiscuity can there be in each individual going into a booth and casting a ballot?" He also asserts that were this a valid argument there would be no end to the matter: "It would be forbidden to walk in the street or to enter a shop, and so forth." This last argument is of course logical, but lacks foresight, since certain haredi rabbis have recently called for segregation of the sexes in shops and on public transport! To the "domestic harmony" argument, i.e., the desire to prevent husbands and wives from arguing over politics, Rabbi Uziel replies: "If so, let us also deny the vote to sons and daughters who live with their parents."

As we can see, many of his arguments are based on common sense, or "*sevarah*" (reasoning) in halakhic terms. Finally, Rabbi Uziel notes that women are not included in a *minyan* (prayer quorum), nor were they counted in the censuses that appear in the Torah. He retorts: "Let us assume for a moment that they are not a part of the community, that they are not to be counted for anything at all. But are they not intelligent beings created in the image of God?" In short, both sexes were created equal, and their right to vote stems from their very creation. This too is reminiscent of the American Declaration of Independence: "that all men are created equal, that they are endowed by their Creator with certain unalienable Rights" – except for the fact that the Declaration of Independence was referring to men only (white male landowners).

Rabbi Uziel then discusses arguments in favor of barring women from running for office. The most weighty argument is based upon the *Sifre* (*Midrash Halakhah* on the book of Deuteronomy), on the verse "you shall surely set a king over you whom the Lord your God chooses": a "king" and not a queen. Maimonides therefore ruled that a woman cannot be appointed to any public office. Of course, those who support this view must explain the cases in which women have nevertheless held roles of public leadership, such as the prophet Deborah. The most common explanation is that at the time (the days of the Judges), due to the pitiful state of the people, no worthier leaders were found, and they were forced to make do with women. The negative *midrashim* on the names Deborah and Huldah express the rabbis' distaste for women as leaders.

None of this prevented Rabbi Uziel from asserting that the prohibition applies only to appointments by the *Sanhedrin*, and not to democratically-elected officials. There is no question that the election of a woman to office would not denigrate public dignity, because her election would be an expression of the will of the public. Thus, based on common democratic rhetoric, traditional sources and common sense, he attempts to convince us that there is no halakhic reason why a woman should not engage in political activity. His arguments convinced religious Zionist circles, but not the *haredim*. Women appear on the National Religious Party's lists for Knesset and local authorities (although not always in realistic slots), and in the past, have represented the party in the Knesset. Parties such as Agudat Yisrael, Shas and Degel Hatorah have no women candidates. On more than one occasion, NRP-*haredi* alliances have collapsed over this very issue.

In the 1980s, when Lea Shakdiel ran for the religious council in Yeruham, her candidacy was rejected by some of the rabbis due to the fact that she is a woman. Shakdiel appealed to the High Court, and Justice Menahem Elon based his ruling in her favor on Rabbi Uziel's response. To the best of my knowledge, Rabbi Uziel never took these ideas any further. It would be interesting however, to consider other possible ramifications. Could today's definition of "public dignity" for example, permit women to be called to the Torah in the synagogue? Can the public "waive" its dignity? Can the public choose a woman to serve as a rabbi, halakhic authority, or rabbinical court judge?

In closing, I would like to explain the meaning of Rabbi Uziel's remark that the question had been "resolved of its own accord." I will do so through another personal story, concerning a conversation I once had with a representative of Agudat Yisrael. During the 1984 general elections, I volunteered to represent one of the parties on a polling-station committee. I had the good fortune to serve as committee chair in Jerusalem's ultra-orthodox Geulah neighborhood. Most of the voters were *haredim*, both men and women. During a lull in the voting, I asked the Agudah representative whether he was familiar with the responses of Rabbis Kook and Uziel to the question of women's suffrage. He confessed that he was not familiar with the material, and added: "It's clear that women should vote. If secular women were to vote and our women were not, our electoral strength would be diminished by 50%!" And that is the main reason that *haredi* women are permitted to vote. Some readers may see something wrong in this, but I would like to say that in my opinion, that is how *Halakhah* works: it helps us navigate between the highest philosophical-theological principles (as expressed by Rabbi Uziel) on the one hand, and realistic, practical needs on the other. I hope that navigation and balance will continue to guide halakhic authorities in the future, in other issues as well, such as the problem of *agunot* (deserted wives) and women who are denied divorce.

Past and Present

History and Culture from a Gender Perspective

"Blessed art Thou, Lord our God, who hast not made me a woman"

RACHEL ELIOR

Over the millennia Jewish tradition has preserved holy scripture, halakhic works, a rich juristic legacy, legends, poetry and liturgy, Kabbalah and homilies. It recalls and sanctifies laws and customs rooted in ancient historical memory, while constantly shaping a complex frame of reference, reflecting its efforts to adapt to changing reality. Looking at the various aspects of Judaism's multifaceted written tradition, one cannot help but notice the striking fact that it was entirely created, written, edited, studied and preserved exclusively by men. In the thousands of volumes that constitute the literary corpus of the "People of the Book," there is not one Hebrew book written, edited or published by a woman prior to the 20th century.

This lacuna is of great significance, because it attests to a decisive fact: Woman have not participated in shaping the norms that have governed their lives, nor have they taken part in the creative cultural process conducted in the public arena, producing the laws, customs, values and standards, and reflecting in legend and *Halakhah*, in story and song, ethics and education, sermon and vision, the foundations of the common space of meaning of a specific cultural community. Moreover, their voices were never heard, their experience not considered, their perspective, aspirations, fears, priorities, unique standards and values, ideas and memories, all were plunged into the abyss of oblivion, absent from written memory.

Women had no part in the Holy Tongue or in the world of education – the fundamental Jewish value of "Torah study" – since they remained within the confines of home and family, excluded from the institutions of learning and kept away from the loci of knowledge and leadership, which were always in the male public domain. Written and spoken Hebrew, which established and defined the legal and cultural space of meaning in which relations between men and women were conducted – by virtue of its status as the Holy Tongue, the language of reading and writing, *Halakhah*, law and ritual, justice and instruction – was created in its written form and preserved in the totality of cultural endeavors, entirely by men. The traditional male view concerning the place of women in the world of study, knowledge and creativity, is reflected in the resounding words of Rabbi Elazar: "May the words of the Torah be burnt rather than given to women" (JT, *Sotah* 3, 4), and in the categorical statement: "he who teaches his daughter Torah, it is as if he has taught her nonsense or indecency" (*Mishnah, Sotah* 3, 4) – establishing a benchmark regarding the general unsuitability of women. Other common sayings restrict the range of female understanding to housework: "A woman's wisdom lies only in the spindle," and a woman's purpose in life to bearing children: "women are solely for the sake of [bearing] children" (*Mishnah, Ketubot* 6). Statements such as these, or for example, "The voice of a woman is indecent" (*Kiddushin* 70a) – which prohibited the active participation of women in all public forums and prevented women from making their voices heard – created a situation of exclusion and a sense of inferiority, reflecting both the theory and practice of the patriarchal order. These excluding voices, present to this day in written and oral teachings, have made their mark on male consciousness through the generations, and have served as justification for a worldview that relegates women to ignorance, confines their wisdom to handicrafts, shuts them up at home, behind the walls of modesty and control, compels them to serve the family, and associates them with concepts of indecency, impurity, subservience and service.

Jewish tradition does not recognize equality between the sexes – as clearly evidenced by the personal status laws reflecting relations between men and women as presented in the Torah, Talmud, Midrash and halakhic literature of all periods. *Halakhah* asserts that "the lives of men take preference over those of women" (*Mishnah, Horayot* 3, 7) – further elaborating upon the nature of relations between men and women from the very beginning: "A rib was taken from Adam, and he was given a handmaiden to serve him" (*Sanhedrin* 39b). Relations between men and women were determined by God's curse to Eve: "and thy desire shall be to thy husband, and he shall rule over thee" (Gen 3:16), interpreted in detail in halakhic literature and rulings governing relations between the sexes: "The fruits of her labors belong to her husband [...] and she must serve him" (Maimonides, *Hilkhot Ishut* 21, 1–4). This perception of the relationship between men and women – master and handmaiden, husband and attendant, lord and serf – sealed the fate of women and sentenced them to a limited existence, the entire essence of which was subordination to male proprietorship – including childbearing, indenture to serve fathers, brothers, husbands and sons, who in turn ensure that "the glory of the king's daughter is within," forbidding women to go out, acquire knowledge and independence, and be sovereign human beings. Subordination to a husband and the satisfaction of his needs were sanctioned by law, and required of women, regardless of their opinions and desires. When necessary. they were even imposed by force: "for a woman who fails to perform any of the tasks required of her, is compelled to do so, even with a whip" (Maimonides, *ibid.*).

Liturgical commentator David Abudraham encapsulates the situation as follows: "a woman is indentured to her husband to fulfill his needs" (*Perush Hatefilot*, p. 25). This concept of enslavement was the deciding factor in determining the status of women, even though wrapped in ceremony and custom, poetry and mythology. It must be acknowledged that the diversity of life was immeasurably greater than that afforded by narrow halakhic definitions; and within the home many Jewish women enjoyed respect and protection, and were far better off than their non-Jewish sisters. However, the patriarchal approach – in all its legal, cultural and social manifestations – held exclusive sway over relations between the sexes, determined the boundaries of role and value, licit and illicit, terms of entry and exit in both private and public domains, freedom and sovereignty, personal status and freedom of expression.

Women were seen as property and tools: as a valuable resource in terms of fertility and continuity, and attendants bound to perform all household chores. They were excluded from the realm of spiritual and intellectual, denied education and freedom, sovereignty, independence and knowledge – in order to enable them to fulfill only their traditional role. Consequently, women were barred from the arena of cultural creativity, public expression, study and knowledge, discussion and debate. For millennia, women were destined to realize only one dimension of their existence – the physical, natural dimension of sex and procreation – and to express themselves only within the confines of the home. In other words, in various societies women were denied dignity, freedom and sovereignty as human beings, perceived rather as the property of their fathers until marriage, and their husbands after marriage. They were denied any existence beyond their bodies and their homes, including spiritual existence and social independence.

These fundamental positions were rooted in law, scripture, myth and behavioral norms, including means of enforcement and punishment. This state of affairs, determined by biological differences and the balance of power between the sexes, was the lot of women in various cultures and religions throughout history, although the manner in which each society defined, established, interpreted and justified it in law, myth, language and custom, varies from culture to culture.

Concern for the continuity and fertility that depended upon the female body, made that body a valuable resource, a desired possession and object of exclusive ownership, guaranteed through legal means that denied women independent existence and sovereignty over their bodies and spirits. According to ancient tradition, the vestiges of which can be seen in various cultures to this day, a woman belongs to her father, from whom she is bought in return for a bride-price, and she pays her husband-redeemer a dowry, and becomes his exclusive property. The talmudic tractate of *Ketubot* puts it succinctly: "A woman is acquired by means of money, contract or cohabitation." This acquisition is the result of commerce between men, at the end of which the woman is transferred from her father's to her husband's domain, taking his name and becoming his property.

In (Hebrew) linguistic memory, women are portrayed as chattel, permanent goods, fertile land, soil, sown earth, Eve, Mother Earth, abundant vines, homes, patrimonies, estates and other realties. Men, on the other hand, appear as land-owners, sowers, farmers, owners of homes, flocks and women. The words "husband" (*ba'al*), "sir" (*adon*), "mister" (*mar*), "man" (*gever*), express the ownership, mastery, lordship and dominance typical of the male condition, and in keeping with the wedding and bedding – acquired through money and sanctioned by law – associated with sowing, fertility and property, and affording control over women's bodies and spirits.

These subject-object relations were instituted in religious law, based on God's words soon after creation: "and thy desire shall be to thy husband, and he shall rule over thee" (Gen 3:16), in which Adam was established as Eve's superior, lord and master. Women's loss of sovereignty and their subjugation as possessions are manifested in divorce proceedings, which are conducted entirely according to the will of the husband and owner, who casts out his possession. According to Jewish religious law, "a man divorces only of his own will, and a woman is divorced against her will" (Mishnah, Yevamot 1, 14) (Rabbi Gershom decreed however, that a woman cannot be divorced against her will). In any event, a woman cannot divorce, but can only be divorced. She cannot act, but can only be acted upon, as she is not a sovereign human being with equal rights, but is rather indentured to her husband, and hence only able to divorce with his consent: "A man who divorces is unlike a woman who divorces, for a woman is divorced willingly or unwillingly, and a man divorces only of his own volition" (*ibid.* 112b).

The clear connection between a woman's exclusive childbearing role and her loss of sovereignty as a human being is stated explicitly in the Talmud: "women are solely for the sake of [bearing] children" (*Mishnah, Kutubot* 6), further declaring that a woman who remains childless for ten years must be divorced (*Mishnah, Yevamot* 64). Responsibility for fertility and infertility, associated with divine grace, is placed entirely upon the woman, and if she is unable to fulfill her destiny, her marriage is pointless, and she is divorced.

This order of things, whereby fathers and husbands are exclusive masters over women and slaves, sheep, cattle and lands, and whereby men head all institutions and control all positions of power, is called patriarchal – from the Latin "*pater*" (father), and is illustrated in the Bible, *Halakhah* and legends. This order, based upon inequality and upon a fundamental cultural and legal distinction between men and women, whereby – as noted above – a woman is subordinate to her husband, and is considered his property, lies at the very core of society and culture throughout the traditional world. It is reflected in metaphorical expressions of the relations between men and women as man to earth, spirit to matter, soul to body, culture to nature. This classification created a distinction between those spheres of activity identified as male – culture and spirit (creative Man) – and those identified as female – nature and the body (created Man). Culture, spirit, creativity and freedom are the exclusive province of men, while nature, the body, passivity and subjugation are the province of women.

Attitudes toward nature, as represented by woman, are ambivalent, as a result of its being the source of life and fertility, beauty and passion, as well as posing mortal danger and threatening the boundaries of culture and human sovereignty. The ambivalence is reflected in the meanings of the Hebrew word "*rehem*" (womb), which signifies both the source of life and the place in which it is created, and a tomb, the place in which life is extinguished (*Mishnah*, *Ohalot* 7, 4; Even Shoshan, *Hamilon Hehadash*, under entry "*kever*"). It is also reflected in the image of Mother Earth, mother of all living things and the source of fertility, as well as the place of interment, to which we return in death. Biology itself reflects this ambivalence, through the involuntary monthly cycle of ovulation, associated with life (pure blood, representing the promise of life and continuity) and death (impure blood, representing the failure to conceive and death). Through this uncontrolled creation and termination, women became associated with the cycle of nature, and were seen at the same time as being different, "other," frightening and mysterious, threatening and helpless, therefore requiring restraint and seclusion, safeguarding and taming, supervision, purification and isolation. Men however, not being subject to any fixed cycle of physiological change, not being connected to the cycle of life and death, and not being subject against their will to nature every month, were seen as powerful and free. Subjection to the cycle of ovulation and creation associated with blood and birth and the eternal cycle of nature, was perceived as weakness and helplessness, since Man has no control over it. This subjection was associated both with the hope and divine blessing of continuity of life ("the blessing of breasts and womb"), and with fear and the curse of heaven, due to the mortal danger involved (infertility and extinction).

This complexity was expressed in religious terms of purity and impurity, indecency and menstrual uncleanness, blessings and curses, affording women ambivalent status with regard to life and death, fertility and extinction.

The relationship between culture and nature became a dialectic of interior and exterior, with women – subject to the cycles of nature – remaining within the protected privacy and modesty of the home, under the protection or subjugation of their husbands; and men – free of subjection to natural cycles and the bonds of subordination, modesty and silence imposed upon women ("the voice of a woman is indecent"; "the glory of the king's daughter lies within"; "a woman should not leave her doorstep") – appropriating the public domain, independence, a voice, speech, education, power and freedom, knowledge and culture, and all of the consequent privileges ("Public," "society" and "community" all refer to the presence of a minimum of ten men. Women are not counted. "The world," "public dignity," "public domain" and "quorum," are all concepts that refer exclusively to men).

Expressions of culture – **language and voice**, law and calendar, letter and number, book and story, sacred and study, knowledge and creativity, judicature and authority, rule and memory – were the province of men. The **silent, voiceless, languageless, letterless, numberless** essence of nature, in all its ambivalence of life and death, blessing and curse, beauty and fertility, seduction, danger and passion, uncleanness and indecency, was associated with women.

Male culture, with its exclusive voice, was associated with power and potency, mastery, taming, government and control, dignity and self-restraint, establishing ownership and order. Expressions of male sexuality identified with power and potency were treated positively and highly regarded: potent-potential (the opposite of impotent), virile, manly, as well as the connection (in Hebrew) between [sexual] desire (*yetzer*) and creation (*yetzirah*).

Female nature on the other hand, was associated with sex and unbridled passion, and uncontrolled female sexuality was identified with indecency and shame, impurity and uncleanness, weakness and disgrace – requiring the sanctification of marriage, purification, immersion and quantification, in order to render it fit for pregnancy and fertility within the realm of ownership and culture. Women's nature was perceived as desirable, threatening and uncontrollable, hence requiring taming and restraining, isolation and modesty, linked as it was with arousal and breach of order. Women – representatives of nature and subject to its cycles – were seen until very recently as objects of control and supervision (modesty, honor), under male authority. The suppression of female sexuality unless under male control, or in the service of fertility within the framework of husband and family, is clearly evident in the linguistic distinctions between indecency, shame, weakness, disgrace, harlot, strumpet, prostitute; and wife – an honorable woman, whose honor is linked to that of her husband, and whose sexuality is sanctified by ritual. It is noteworthy that the derogatory terms referring to female sexuality (in Hebrew) have no masculine equivalents.

The patriarchal approach lies at the root of the social order in many cultures. The treatment of women that derives from this approach may be variously explained and interpreted as a punishment for some sin, as measures taken for their own good and protection, or as representing values of honor and modesty. All such societies however, have been equally coercive in its application. Women were restricted to the confines of their own bodies, homes and families, bound by the shackles of modesty and family honor, prevented from coming and going as they pleased, acquiring an education, sharing in the joy of study, engaging in various fields of activity, realizing their individual talents and abilities, taking on roles of public leadership, jurisprudence and legislation, and being a part of public decision-making.

The fact that such concepts as *"tana," "amora," "hakham," "rabbi," "dayan," "sofer," "talmid hakham," "ga'on," "parnas,"* and the like, have no feminine equivalents in the ancient Hebrew language attests to the absence of women from spiritual and communal life. These roles and the values associated with them were the exclusive province of men, deriving from the sphere of study or communal affairs, and from freedom and sovereignty within the Jewish world, of which women never had the benefit. The value concepts associated with women were "virgin," "modest," "proper," "abundant vine," "woman of valor... the fruits of her labors belong to her husband," "joyful mother of children," "a woman's honor is within," "a help mate for him," and so forth – relating to modesty, pregnancy and fertility, property controlled by the husband, compliance with the social order.

Women had no public voice, their opinions were not considered when it came to matters outside the home. They were barred from the study halls and the religious courts, schools and synagogues (except for the "women's gallery," which confines and isolates women from the precinct in which the ritual is performed). They were not allowed to vote or be elected to office, testify in court, discuss and dispute with others. Women could not go and come as they pleased, and they were unable to acquire knowledge, authority and status. They were little more than still lifes, "as a sheep before her shearers is dumb," "a woman of valor" managing her household and serving her husband – who would recite the blessing "Blessed art thou, Lord our God, who hast not made me a woman" every morning, following the blessing "who hast not made me a slave."

Throughout history, women have been present-absent, nameless, voiceless and unrecorded. Memory was exclusively male, while women were destined to oblivion and anonymity, their existence confined to the ownership of their bodies and their ability to bear a son to carry on their husband's name. This attitude to women is apparent throughout the ages, from "the book of the generations of Adam" (Gen 5), which recounts how men begat men, without a single woman worthy of mention by name for many generations; through the wife of Noah, the wife of Manoah, the daughter of Jephtah, the concubine in Gibeah, the wife of Job, Lot's wife, Lot's daughters, the great woman of Shunem, and the wise woman of Tekoah – all anonymous women, lacking names and existence in their own right, referred to by the name of a father, husband, or place, whose stories are told from a male perspective, and not in their own voices, their experiences wiped out and their names lost in the depths of oblivion; to the lists of founding fathers and pioneers in the Palestine colonies, which enumerate the founding fathers, farmers and pioneers, but ignore the founding mothers.

Such is also the case in many other areas: women are absent from books and libraries, memorials and chronicles, lists of the enfranchised, of elected and appointed officials, of persons of authority and eligibility, of leaders, laureates and title-holders, certain political parties and many religious institutions.

Were such things merely a matter of history, we might simply have speculated upon the scope of this historical wrong and the extent of social injustice, closing with an expression of shock and sorrow at the loss incurred by excluding half of the human race from the public domain, from the arena of knowledge and education, creativity and leadership, freedom and sovereignty. However, despite the decisive change in the status of women in the first half of the 20th century, when they were deemed worthy of education, independence, equality and sovereignty in the eyes of the law, there are still significant areas of life that have retained the stamp of the patriarchal order.

Contemporary Israeli society, perceived as modern and committed to the principles of liberal and egalitarian democracy, in many ways continues to conduct its affairs in an atmosphere dominated by past traditions, wholly unacquainted with the concept of equality between the sexes. The Jewish religion, which reflects a male perspective of reality, plays a crucial role in Israeli social interaction and political discourse, and takes a central place in gender relations – contingent upon the personal status laws that affect the entire population. Religious family law applies to all permanent residents of Israel, according to the respective rites of the various religious communities, regardless of personal beliefs or lifestyles. The personal status laws which govern marriage, divorce, levirate marriage, deserted wives and women who are denied divorce, questions of assets, inheritance, financial relations and property rights in the context of marriage and its dissolution – thus apply to all women in Israel, religious and secular alike. They are all subject to patriarchal methods of determining their personal status, since the norms in this area were established and continue to be established by various religious methods exercised by exclusively male institutions. Women are thus unable to participate in the process of determining the norms to which they themselves are subject.

It is not only the law pertaining to relations between the sexes however, that is influenced by religious-patriarchal mores, but also a significant part of the surrounding culture, since the Hebrew language – imbued with Jewish concepts and traditional culture – forges the world view that directly and indirectly affects gender relations. The language embodies social values and sustains thought patterns and lifestyles. All speakers of Hebrew – which developed as a language, culture, religion and world of meaning, both explicit and implicit, over thousands of years, within the confines of traditional society – are heirs to religious, patriarchal thought, whether they know it or not. The legacy of patriarchal thought can be found in all areas of language, in varied written and spoken expressions, in law and convention, custom and imagery, manifest culture and hidden expectations, in the fundamental perceptions of sanctity and life, in association and in myth. All of these things affect the field of meaning established in personal and public life, and the balance of power between the various parts of society, as well as individual and general conduct with regard to sovereignty, freedom and equality.

Expressions and terms that reflect an unequal, male-dominated and male-oriented perception, such as: "the voice of a woman is indecent"; "blessed art thou, who hast not made me a woman"; "I find women more bitter than death"; "a woman is acquired by means of money, contract or cohabitation"; "he hath found some uncleanness in her"; "virginal blood"; "divorcée"; "a woman is divorced willingly or unwillingly, and a man divorces only of his own volition"; "deserted wife"; "divorce-denied woman"; "housewife"; "battered woman" and many others – reflect contemporary reality, and not just past eras. In many areas of life, women are still denied equal rights and opportunities for sovereignty, freedom and dignity, a share in responsibility and a fair division of rights and obligations, joint property, resources and advantages. The absence of women in many fields clearly proves the continuing pattern of present-absenteeism, whereby women are present when it comes to home and family, but absent from the sphere of spiritual and creative pursuits, culture and leadership. The absence of women judges in the rabbinical courts, before which their personal status is decided; their absence in the *yeshivot*, in which the fundamental norms of the religious world are dis-cussed; their absence in the public performance of ritual; their absence among those counted for a prayer quorum; their complete absence in the *haredi* political leadership (there are no women on the Haredi parties such as Shas or UTJ Knesset lists); their absence in positions of rabbinical authority and instruction, as well as social and professional functions in the religious world, from halakhic authorities to religious court judges, from *kashruth* supervisors and circumcisers to community leaders; their absence in the military-defense leadership and in many roles in the IDF and security services; the small number of women in the government and Knesset; the small number of women mayors and women in various leadership tracks; their small number among the country's economic leaders; their small number at the highest levels of academia – as compared with their decisive presence among low-wage-earners, recipients of National Insurance benefits, and their infinitely high number among the victims of violence, illustrates the influence exercised by the old norms.

Even today, in many places, women are concealed and ex-cluded from the public domain, through various modesty laws: in certain communities and institutions, they are still prevented from voting or being elected; they are still barred from many jobs; and in many institutions, they may neither teach nor study. They are still forbidden to make their voices heard in religious public for reasons of "public dignity," and they are not allowed to go out without a veil, head-covering or wig, or to wear clothing deemed "immodest" by men. A significant number of Israeli women are denied educa-tion (for example, among Beduin, rural Muslim communities and *haredi* communities in which girls are restricted to all-girl institu-tions) and freedom of movement (*haredi* society does not allow women to learn to drive, and restricts the movements of girls). Integration into society and the ability to choose a profession are naturally limited when women are denied sovereignty over their bodies and spirits, and when limitations are imposed upon their access to education, freedom of movement and freedom of expres-sion. This is not about a specific community or prohibition, but about society as a whole, based on an assessment of the role of women in making decisions that affect their lives, their level of participation in finance, power and religious authority, the kind of access they have to the public arena, and the amount of influence they exert on processes of change in various areas of traditional and modern life.

In recent decades, many of these spheres of activity have witnessed a revolution, inspired by changes in the West regarding such concepts as human dignity, liberty and equality, and influenced by cultural pluralism, which recognizes the multiplicity of values, tastes and lifestyles that reflect the variety of human experience. In the religious world, women have begun to study, and to criticize the basic concepts that have determined the relationship between the private and the public domains, the inside and the outside. In the secular world, an increasing number of women are studying, taking part in education and cultural criticism, changing fundamental patriarchal and sexist values in many fields. Education, freedom and equality, and their incorporation in legislation have expanded the meaning of human dignity and liberty, making it possible to take part in public, cultural, social and professional activities striving to extend the boundaries of liberal-humanist thought, recognizing equality between the different, and not just equality between the like.

Men and women who oppose the traditional patriarchal norms must examine the roots of these norms, as well as their various expressions in law and practice, while critically assessing the presence and absence of women of all aspects of life, in every field, and the influence women exert in effecting change and in the decision-making process. They must seek out that which requires change, and act to achieve greater equality, deeper human dignity, sovereignty and freedom for all who are created in God's image.

Linguistic, legal, religious and cultural criticism, as well as an understanding of the interaction between them – as reflected in custom, *Halakhah*, the religious courts, ceremony, and daily language, vis-à-vis precincts of permitted and forbidden presence, voice and silence; defining the boundaries of the sacred and that which is taken for granted in the traditional world, as well as a significant part of the prevailing norms in the modern world – sharpen awareness of the existing disparity between theoretical recognition of the right of women to equality and freedom, sovereignty and dignity, and its practical application.

Feminism as *Tikkun Ha-Olam*

LEA SHAKDIEL

Progressive Jews have been using the term *"tikkun olam"* ever since the idealistic awakening of the 1960s in the United States and in Western Europe. It is identified periodically with commitment to morally worthy causes, in keeping with the *Zeitgeist*: inter-racial solidarity, world peace, the war against poverty, and naturally, feminism too. This trend comprises a number of elements:

First, it is a creative response to the death of direct faith in God and in the myths of traditional religion, and the secularization of life. Naive faith was replaced by the cult of freedom and individual self-fulfillment, but this failed to satisfy the need for a sanctuary from alienation, loneliness and helplessness, the need to ground our lives within a framework of meaning that transcends the concrete, the personal, the here and now. If the transcendental cannot be experienced through devotion to the divine, it can still be experienced through devotion to "the spirit of man," in keeping with the humanistic ideal of a rational humanity lighting our path from ancient times to the endless reaches of the future. This belief in "the pedagogy of potential Man in real society"[1] gives us the

---

[1] This is the brilliant title of an article by humanistic educator Z. Lamm, about another humanistic educator, C. Frankenstein, 1985. *Megamot* 29, 2, pp. 123–127. (Hebrew)

strength to take concrete action to repair a defective reality, to build a better world for our children. In other words, *"tikkun olam"* is perceived today as a version of personal and universal redemption, open to various agnostics and atheists as well: "For yet I shall believe in Man/ And in his spirit, a spirit bold."[2]

Feminism is thus no more than an upgraded version of humanism.[3] We decry the prevailing tendency to identify the abstract concept of "the rational human spirit" exclusively with men, and affirm that Man is a sexed being, with a mind that reflects the best of both male and female. Will it be "He and I" only who "will change the world," to quote the words of Arik Einstein – one of the most prominent representatives of the Sabra myth? Kalanit Dover, for example, amended this to "She and I will change the world," as the slogan for "Nissan," a leadership training project she started for high-school girls. This is, fundamentally, Liberal Feminism: a philosophy that accepts the social contract as chartered by modern liberal democracy, while demanding that the female half of humanity be allowed to participate on equal footing, both in the struggle to attain its goals, and in the division of the spoils and fruits of its labor.

Second, adopting the term *"tikkun olam"* from Jewish sources offers Jews of various beliefs – religious, traditional, secular – a fine solution to the problems of identity that have plagued us all since the assertion that "our nation is not a nation except by virtue of its divine laws," to quote Sa'adiah Ga'on, lost its predominance. We can celebrate our humanity, our acceptance into the family of "normal" nations, as one more nuance of universal culture, without ceding our Jewish self-perception, rooted in our specific historical

---

[2] S. Tchernichowsky, 1894. "Credo" [Ani Ma'amin], Odessa. Published in *Mivhar Shirim*, Dvir, 1965, pp. 169–170. (Hebrew)

[3] P. Johnson, 1994. *Feminism as Radical Humanism*, Westview Press, Boulder.

tradition. Hence the strong emphasis Reform Judaism has placed since its inception, not only upon a messianic-eschatological approach to modernism and progress, but also upon identifying the goals of the French Revolution with "the ethics of the Prophets": We too have an ancient humanistic classical tradition, that confers on us honorary membership among the founders of liberal democracy.[4] How good it is to recall for example, that one of our own, Rene Cassin, drafted the United Nations' Declaration of Human Rights!

All of this was expressed in European languages, until the gradual return of the various streams of liberal Judaism to the sources of their national culture and identity. In our generation we are thus experiencing a change of direction.[5] Instead of repairing Jews and Judaism under the foreign banner (borrowed obviously from the history of the Church) of "Reform," as necessary self-renovation toward acceptance in the modern world – the colors of *"tikkun olam"* are now proudly flown – in Hebrew – as the mantra of an ethnic rite in the Holy Tongue, reconnecting Jews to their roots. *"Tikkun olam"* is not merely an abstract ideal, but a resounding semantic code, like the songs around the tribal fire – the convocational platform of a community of believers. One such community was founded by Michael Lerner, around *Tikkun Magazine*, which he edits, and thereby strives to develop a "politics of mean-

---

[4] For example, "The Pittsburgh Platform 1885," in M. Meyer, 1988. *Response to Modernity: A History of the Reform Movement in Judaism,* Oxford University Press.

[5] M. Graetz claims that such a reverse trend has been in evidence for a number of generations: "Secular Messianism in the 19th Century as a Way of Returning to Judaism," in Z. Baras (ed.), 1984. *Messianism and Eschatology [Meshihiyut Ve-Eschatologia],* Merkaz Zalman Shazar, pp. 401–418 (Hebrew).

ing" in face of the threats posed by the destructive global age in which we live.[6]

We owe the popularity of the term itself almost certainly to Gershom Scholem and Martin Buber: to Scholem – for promulgating the Lurianic concepts of *Tsimtsum-Shevirath Ha-Kelim – Tikkun*;[7] and to Buber – for his monumental project dedicated to promoting Hassidism as a means of individual and collective therapy for Jews disillusioned with the failed dream of Emancipation.[8] The Lurianic myth provides the essential symbolism required by any active vision, and indeed serves mostly as an aesthetic-literary ornament to the philosophy of present-day "world-fixers." For content, however, they resorted to the Hassidic concept of *"tikkun,"* inasmuch as it is far more open and vague than its predecessors, and therefore easier for a generation of assertive, free and sovereign Jews to embrace. It is a modest and partial *"tikkun"* that enables every individual to participate in daily acts of charity in the immediate surroundings, linking this simple action to a communal and world-wide effort, without making the value attached to such action contingent upon effecting a drastic change in lifestyle, history, or the cosmos. There is no need for greater observance of

---

[6] See for example, M. Lerner, 1999. "Globalization of Spirit vs. The Globalization of Capital," paper presented at Ben-Gurion University in the International Seminar: Challenging the Nation-State – Perspectives on Citizenship and Identity; A. Arkush (1997), *"Realism and Idealism in Recent American Jewish Political Thought – Lerner, Boyarin, Wisse,"* paper presented at Bar-Ilan University in a conference on Jewish Political Thought.

[7] That is, contraction of divine light into vessels, the explosion of those vessels so that the light disperses into sparks, and the repairing brought about when those sparks are redeemed. G. Scholem, 1974. *The Messianic Idea in Judaism and Other Essays on Jewish Spirituality*, New York, Schocken.

[8] A. Shapira, 1991. "Repairing Oneself and Repairing the World According to Buber," *Da'at* 27: 61–71 (Hebrew).

religious precepts, donating all of one's possessions to the poor, or even leading the Jewish People out of exile: It is both possible and imperative to improve the quality of personal, moral, political and spiritual life.

Feminists who join this aspect of Jewish renaissance in our generation, strive to ground the women's revolution not only in the necessary "*tikkun*" of the political and economic balance of power, but primarily in effecting a perceptual and cultural change in both women and men, as human beings and as Jews reinterpreting a rich and complex heritage. This effort goes beyond the mandate adopted by Liberal Feminism: Paradoxically this Radical Feminism is more traditional than its moderate forerunner.

One example of this is the surprising address made by Prof. Laura Brown at the American Psychological Association's award ceremony.[9] Brown rained fire and brimstone upon many of her colleagues, who had in her opinion betrayed the fundamental mission of their profession: placing their expertise at the exclusive disposal of their clients, and devoting themselves to helping others within the context of the struggle for a more just society. She noted that her position had developed within the three movements for social change to which she belonged: the feminist movement; the gay rights movement; and the movement for adult survivors of childhood interpersonal violence. Brown combines all of this with memories of her *bat-mitzvah* at a Conservative synagogue, her own interpretation of Ezekiel's Vision of the Dry Bones, and frequent use of the Hebrew words "*tikkun olam.*" She also returns the Marxist concept of self-alienation to its Jewish roots, and grounds psychological alienation in the myth of "exile and redemption," with faint echoes of Lurianic Kabbalah, naturally.

---

[9] L.S. Brown, 1997. "The Private Practice of Subversion: Psychology as Tikkun Olam," *American Psychologist*, vol. 52 no. 4, April, pp. 449–462.

The most systematic contribution to the development of the link between Jewish feminism and "*tikkun olam*" is undoubtedly that of philosopher and theologian Judith Plaskow. Her book, *Standing Again at Sinai – Judaism from a Feminist Perspective*,[10] although a collection of articles published over the years, forms a cohesive whole, culminating in the final chapter: "Feminist Judaism and *Tikkun Ha-Olam.*"[11] Plaskow stresses the fact that the "*tikkun*" in question derives from Judaism's "*ortho-praxis*" – a correct way of life, appropriate behavior; as opposed to Christianity's emphasis upon "*ortho-doxa*" – correct belief. It is interesting that a progressive American Jew like Plaskow attained such a level of admiration for the centrality of *Halakhah* in Judaism, indirectly – from "Liberation Theology," a neo-Marxist revolutionary Christian doctrine that advocates mobilizing religion for political struggles on behalf of the poor and the oppressed of the world. The connection between the traditional significance of *Halakhah* and the feminist action advocated by Plaskow, perhaps resembles the connection between *Halakhah* and the Zionist-pioneer emphasis on "*hagshamah*"[12] as a timely "religious" imperative. In other words, we have here a new hermeneutic approach to Judaism, and as intimated by the book's title, an invitation to renew the covenant between Jews and their ancient heritage. In another important article,[13] Plaskow reinter-

---

[10] J. Plaskow, 1990. *Standing Again at Sinai – Judaism from a Feminist Perspective*, Harper, San Francisco, chapter 6, esp. p. 214.

[11] *Sic* in the title. Throughout the text however, she employs the term "*tikkun olam*," like others of her generation. More on this below.

[12] That is, applying oneself in person to the attainment of Zionist goals in the land of Israel; literally, "materialization" (of an abstract ideal).

[13] "Jewish Theology in Feminist Perspective," in: L. Davidman and S. Tenenbaum (eds.), 1994. *Feminist Perspectives on Jewish Studies*, Yale University Press, pp. 62–84.

prets "theology" as the welding together of Jewish identity and a *weltanschauung* that dictates concrete action for feminist *"tikkun olam."* God would thus appear to be no more than the focusing idea behind redemptive human action – a kind of theology open to the religious and the secular alike, as long as they are committed to an active Jewish-feminist identity.

As a Zionist, I am saddened by the dichotomy characteristic of Israeli society: at one end of the spectrum, a secular elite alienated from its Jewish heritage; at the other end, religious Jews opposed to any value tainted by universalism (God forbid); and in the middle, a lot of rather confused "ordinary Jews." Spiritual revival is identified exclusively with fundamentalism, dangerous messianism and religious coercion, and not with ethical-social protest. We therefore find it difficult to see what is to be gained by applying the discourse of *"tikkun olam"* to the struggle to eradicate all forms of violence and discrimination against women, for example. How many of us would indeed feel motivated to action – beyond merely ratifying the appropriate international convention[14] – by such harmony between the particular and the universal in our cultural identity?

When Purim of 1998 was approaching, another feminist theologian, Bonna Haberman, suggested that the Fast of Esther be dedicated to the struggle against the sale of women into the slavery of prostitution throughout the world, including Israel. The suggestion seemed reasonable to the liberal Jewish community in the United States: They loved the idea of appropriating the Jewish queen who turned from a sex object into a springboard for national salvation. In Israel on the other hand, secular feminists responded to the idea by immediately pigeonholing it as "religious": Femi-

---

[14] CEDAW – Convention on the Elimination of all Forms of Discrimination Against Women, Conventions 1035, vol. 31, *Rashumot.* The 1979 convention was ratified by Israel in 1991.

nism, they thought, needed to relate to tradition only in the sense of "know thy enemy."[15]

A new stream has recently joined the ranks of Jewish feminism: Orthodox feminism. Often treated as a partial, late and reluctant imitation of its more progressive forerunners, little innovation is expected of it.

Thus for example, Dr. Susan Aranoff[16] – citing Conservative feminist talmudic scholar Prof. Judith Hauptman[17] – stresses the fact that the term *"tikkun olam"* comes from the *Mishnah*, *Gittin* chapters 4-5, where it is used to justify changes in *Halakhah* based on flexible and creative interpretations, aimed at correcting injustices, and providing assistance to victims of problematic legal mechanisms with morally undesirable consequences. The editor of the *Mishnah* chose to place this varied list (freeing slaves, ransoming captives, etc.) in the tractate of *Gittin*, beginning with a law pertaining to women: Rabbi Gamliel the Elder discontinued the hitherto acceptable Halakhic practice whereby a husband who had sent a writ of divorce to his wife by messenger, might recant, convene another religious court, and declare before that court that the writ of divorce en route is no longer valid. Hauptman interprets this Halakhic amendment as evidence of the Rabbis' tendency to treat weak groups with justice and compassion: Rabbi Gamliel's intention was to release *"agunot"* (deserted wives). He therefore ruled

---

[15] Correspondence on e-mail listserves Women's Tefilla Network, Bridges, and Israeli Feminist Forum, Winter 1998. Data on the criminal traffic in women and the efforts to combat it can be found in a detailed report by the Israel Women's Network.

[16] S. Aranoff, B. Marcus and L. Shakdiel, 1998. "Feminism as Tikkun Olam," Closing Ceremony, *Second International Conference on Feminism and Orthodoxy*, February 16, New York, Tape.

[17] J. Hauptman, 1998. "Annulment of Marriage," in *Rereading the Rabbis, A Woman's Voice*, Westview Press, Boulder, pp. 110–114.

that a husband may not torment his wife by canceling a divorce he had already agreed to grant. Aranoff has adopted this interpretation, and made it a cornerstone of the ongoing struggle of religious feminists to convince today's rabbinical establishment to be more flexible regarding the laws of divorce, and to find an immediate solution to the fundamental problem of divorce as a unilateral legal action that places all of the power in the hands of men. Aranoff asserts that the danger to the sanctity of marriage lies not in amending *Halakhah*, but in perpetuating the present state of affairs: the rabbis' refusal to assure women that marriage is not a trap.

According to this approach, the concept of *"tikkun olam"* remains within the framework of Liberal Feminism's striving toward a more egalitarian Judaism and the gradual elimination of the vestiges of patriarchal discrimination against women. The Talmudic scholars among us have but to apply their skills to elucidating Jewish sources from the Bible to the present, without expecting to find any new insight into *"tikkun olam"* or feminism. It sounds a little like the claim of Reform and other Jews since the beginning of the *Haskalah* – almost 200 years late: Judaism has been overcome by fossilized clericalism; it has lost its dynamic vitality; we are in danger of mass desertion, and the state of our women is the acid test of the entire system. Many years after the poignant cry "Hebrew woman, who knows your life?…,"[18] we Orthodox women are finally becoming convinced that these complaints are justified, but our restraint is apparent: We seek to work only within the framework of *Halakhah* – with the rabbis, not against them.

I would like to suggest another possible contribution of Orthodox feminism to the discussion of *"tikkun olam,"* based on this movement's two ontological premises: Belief in a God-given Torah even when it is experienced as the androcentric creation of a God

---

[18] J.L. Gordon, 1905. *"Kotzo shel Yod," Poetry in Six Books, book 4 – Epic Poems*, Hatzfirah, Warsaw, pp. 5–50 (Hebrew).

often described in male terms;[19] and insistence upon "feminism of gender difference" (i.e., equal value of different roles, gender identities, and unique and separate cultural and spiritual creativity), rather than "feminism of equality."[20]

The first premise insists upon a unity of God, truth, and objective reality; while the second premise asserts a multiplicity of human manifestations. Combined, these two premises enable epistemological pluralism, a dynamic variety of paths to God, Torah interpretation and ritual, including diverse gender forms. If Modernism provided a "window of opportunity" for "Liberal-progressive Jewish Feminism," Postmodernism – which we share with Radical Feminists – has provided here another "window of opportunity."

A disclaimer: I believe that Yossef Ahituv was right in cautioning against extreme Postmodernism, which is essentially complete value relativism, and the disintegration of human discourse into a cacophony of autistic babble. This kind of Postmodernism leaves no room for *"tikkun olam,"* since by

---

[19] T. Ross and Y. Gelman, 1998. "The Implications of Feminism for Orthodox Jewish Theology," in: Menahem Mautner, Avi Sagi and Ronen Shamir (eds.), *Multiculturalism in a Democratic Jewish State: Memorial Volume for Prof. Ariel Rosen-Zvi*, Ramot, Tel-Aviv University, pp. 443–464 (Hebrew); T. Ross, 1999. "Can Women Still Pray to God the Father?," in: N. Ilan (ed.), *Dialogue and Polemic in Jewish Culture, A Jubilee Volume for Tova Ilan*, Hakibbutz Hameuhad and Ne'emanei Torah Va'avodah, pp. 264–277 (Hebrew). T. Ross, 2000. "Modern Orthodoxy and the Challenge of Feminism," in: J. Frankel (ed.), *Jews and Gender, the Challenge to Hierarchy*, Studies in Contemporary Jewry, an annual, XVI, The Harman Institute of Contemporary Jewry, The Hebrew University of Jerusalem, pp. 3–38, esp. pp. 25–27.

[20] R. Lubitch, 1997. "What is Women's Place?," *Amudim, Av-Elul*, pp. 322–326 (Hebrew).

definition, one person's repair is another's disrepair.[21]

The feminist project has thus often reached an impasse: the empowerment of different women may lead to a kind of multi-cultural approach, whereby all female experiences around the world are of equal value, precluding the ability to define oppression and liberation, and the difference between the world before and after its repair.[22] One disturbing example that comes to mind is female genital mutilation – performed by women on girls in certain cultures, and justified by many women in the name of ethnic feminism.

Feminism could adopt a more moderate form of Postmodernism, sometimes termed "constructive."[23] This is a complex attempt to have our cake and eat it too: on the one hand, accepting the fundamental unity of humanity and the world (and in the case of Jewish-religious feminism, also the fundamental unity of God), ascribing eternal, cosmic significance to the sum total of human actions striving for *tikkun olam*; while on the other hand, insisting upon a composite federative approach of multiplicity within unity.

I will illustrate my point with an alternative reading of the *Mishnah* in *Gittin*: It is not the suffering of *agunot* that brought Rabbi Gamliel to change the *Halakhah*, but the fear that a woman might marry another in the interval between receipt of the divorce

[21] Y. Ahituv, 1996. "Repairing Man and Repairing the World in Jewish Texts and in General Culture," Gilayon (*Ne'emanei Torah Va'avodah*), *Kislev*, pp. 16–25 (Hebrew).

[22] S.M. Okin, 1999. *Is Multiculturalism Bad for Women? Susan Moller Okin with Respondents*, eds. J. Cohen, M. Howard and M.C. Nussbaum, Princeton University Press.

[23] S. Kepnes, 1996. "Postmodern Interpretations of Judaism: Deconstructive and Constructive Approaches," in: *Interpreting Judaism in a Postmodern Age*, ed. S. Kepnes, New York University Press, pp. 1–20.

and its withdrawal by her husband, since such a liaison with another man might lead to the birth of *mamzerim*.[24] After all, according to this very *mishnah*, even after the change in *Halakhah*, a
husband may torment his *agunah* wife by physically delaying the
messenger, or physically approaching the wife before the messenger's arrival, and informing her that the writ of divorce is no longer
valid. *"Tikkun olam"* is in fact the bold arrogance of the Rabbis, as a
"serving elite," in presuming to define the desired social order for
the entire people, since people tend to see only their own personal
suffering as requiring redress and redemption, while leaders differ
from the masses in their ability to see society's general, objective
and lasting interest. This overall responsibility is especially evident
in cases when leaders dare to rise above the ordinary legal system,
in order to make "adjustments," designed to enable the system to
continue to function.[25] The use of the term *"tikkun olam"* in reference to this task, was probably influenced by the Hellenistic concept of *"oikoumene"*[26] – which saw the part of the world that the
Greeks had succeeded in conquering and to which they had
brought culture as they saw it, as the entire civilized world; and
everything beyond as "barbarian." The Rabbis wished to "repair" –
i.e., to establish and sustain – a Jewish *"oikoumene"* – a project taken

---

[24] That is, children born of forbidden liaisons and therefore forbidden
forever from marrying legitimate Jews. H. Albek, *Commentary on the
Mishnah*, Order *Nashim*, Tractate *Gittin*, Dvir, p. 281 (Hebrew).

[25] G.J. Blidstein, 1991. "The Import of Early Rabbinic Writings for an
Understanding of Judaism in the Hellenistic-Roman Period," in: S.
Talmon (ed.), *Jewish Civilisation in the Hellenistic-Roman Period*, Sheffield
JSOT Press, pp. 64–72.

[26] Literally: household.

up by all subsequent Halakhists:[27] Man ("microcosm") was created in God's image in order to imitate the divine macrocosm, to distinguish between light and darkness, order and chaos.

A cautious reading of the *mishnah* compels us to bring the definite article back into our discussion: the original text reads "*tikkun **ha**-olam*" (repairing **the** world) and not just "*tikkun olam*,"[28] since everything depends on the essential concentric compatibility between divine-cosmic harmony and the stable social order, or in philosophical terms – identifying the worthy and the good with ontological truth. Although human complications and their repair occur within history, the order itself is perceived as a-historical, eternal and universal, as the nature of the world. Since human beings fit into this world order, repairing the world will in the end also result in redemption from individual suffering. The point of departure however, is not personal suffering, but the comprehensive vision of the leaders, those with power, the "authors of the discourse" itself.[29]

This reading of the *mishnah* seems to me more correct than the comforting optimism Hauptman and Aranoff discover in these founding texts, and therefore it also compels me to find within them another kind of feminism, more conservative, but paradoxically also more radical than theirs. I embrace the Rabbis' presumption to repair **the** world, although I believe their perspective of **the** world was limited by their unconscious androcentrism. It is as if we

---

[27] M. Lorberbaum, 1995. "Tikkun Olam According to Maimonides: A Study of the Teleology of Halakha," *Tarbitz* 64a (*Tishrei-Kislev*), pp. 65–82 (Hebrew).

[28] The source of this common error may be the second paragraph of the *Aleinu* prayer, which reads "*letaken olam bemalkhut shadai.*" Maimonides used the precise term as it appears in the *Mishnah*: "*letaken ha-olam*" – *Mishneh Torah, Shoftim, Hilkhot Melakhim,* 3, 10; 11, 4; etc.

[29] The term *auteurs du discours* was coined by Michel Foucault.

have been trying to repair "the world" with only one eye open, and only now do we open the other eye – that of female perception. "The world" thus changes from exclusive to inclusive, enriched by the addition in scope as well as depth. I do not seek to replace the male picture of the world (e.g., ethic of rights and competition) with another, feminist view (ethic of care and co-operation),[30] but to expand the world's scope manyfold, by adding feminist goals to the repertoire of traditional *"tikkun."* In any event, it is a *"tikkun,"* i.e., the institution of the desired improvement into lasting regularities, taken by women and men beyond the point of no return, and not temporary pain-relief. Generally speaking, this approach is closer to that of the radical Plaskow than to that of the liberal Aranoff. In practical terms, it also accommodates "Orthodox Jewish ortho-praxis."

I will conclude with an interpretation I heard from Orthodox Rabbi Yoel Bin-Nun: The only place in the Torah in which God refers to Himself in the plural is in the context of the plurality of gender at the time of creation: "And God said, Let Us make man in Our image, after Our likeness: and let them have dominion over the fish of the sea[...]. So God created man in His image, in the image of God created He him; male and female created He them. And God blessed them, and God said unto them, Be fruitful, and multiply, and replenish the earth, and subdue it [...]. And God said, Behold I have given you [plural] every herb bearing seed[...] to you [plural] it shall be for meat" (Gen 1:26–29). Feminist repair of the world, therefore, is expressed in developing the ability to include gender plurality within the fundamental unity of God, and conse-

---

[30] For example, C. Gilligan, 1982. *In a Different Voice*, Harvard University, Cambridge, Mass.

quently also within the fundamental unity of humanity and its redemptive action in the world.

The *Minyan*: Gender and Democracy

CHANA SAFRAI

Gender equality is without a doubt a formative, basic and fundamental value in democratic thought. There cannot be democracy
unless it is founded upon the principle of equality for all citizens –
men and women alike – with direct and identical access to all
departments of state, and equal right to participate in the process
of government. A truly democratic society bears the standard of
equality as a formative value in all its endeavors, and is committed
to equality in every aspect of life. Every egalitarian society grapples
with the existence of sub-societies that espouse traditional, religious or other non-egalitarian ideologies. Various democratic
societies have resolved this conflict through separation of church
and state, or non-involvement in religious or sectarian affairs.

My intention here is not to address the basic issue of interaction or clashes between societies with divergent guiding principles,
but to examine the case of a single society comprising both ex-
tremes: the democratic principle, as well as an opposing religious
orientation. In Israel, this phenomenon can be observed in the
society we call "religious-Zionist"; and more so within the reality
termed "secular," which alternately engages "Orthodox" institutions and organizations, imitates them and conforms to established
traditions.

For example, I would cite the emotional appeal by Blu Greenberg in her book *On Women and Judaism*.[1] It is the appeal of women who belong to the same society, and the way they feel when they enter a synagogue in which there are nine men waiting for a quorum, and "only" a woman walks in; the fallen faces and disappointment a woman encounters when she comes to pray with the community, because she is "superfluous," since she is not a man required for worship. In this article, I am not standing up for women, but for Jewish justice.

Another story: Recently, while visiting one of the secular kibbutzim, I attended the local synagogue on a Saturday morning. When the time came to read from the Torah, there appeared to be in the synagogue, two or three guests, a few elderly kibbutz members, and myself – a total of ten people. One of the kibbutz members had to make a telephone call (despite the Sabbath-desecration it entailed), in order to convince another member to come and complete a quorum. The latter agreed, hopped on his bicycle (which also entailed a possible Sabbath-desecration), and rushed to the rescue of men unable to pray as a "community."

I am not discussing my own feelings, as a lecturer who had come to the kibbutz to speak about the weekly portion of the Torah, yet was invisible in the synagogue. It is rather a sense of commitment to equality that I would like to emphasize. How is it possible that those kibbutz members, dedicated to equality as a core value in their lives, or the judges visiting the kibbutz, did not see this as an affront to their democratic principles? Why did the kibbutz feel it was necessary to adopt a non-egalitarian model? Would it not have been preferable to adopt other models of Jewish public life?

---

[1] B. Greenberg, 1981. *On Women and Judaism: A View from Tradition*, Philadelphia, Jewish Publication Society.

Their choice to follow ingrained halakhic tradition would appear to prove that seemingly anti-traditional solutions will not satisfy this or similar groups of worshipers. The question I would like to pose is not whether alternative Conservative or Reform models should be adopted, since one cannot decide which religious framework would be suitable for another. Even I, despite my anger and frustration, do not choose, for my own reasons, to adopt one of the alternatives that have been a part of Jewish reality for quite some time.[2] The issue at hand is a reassessment of the legitimacy of other solutions – without giving in to the hostility with which any reform in this matter would certainly be met. Is it possible to claim, entirely within the framework of *Halakhah*, that full participation of women is or was at one time acceptable, thereby providing justification for a renewed look at whether it should be re-applied, in light of the democratic values that are a part of the world of its adherents?

In research and tradition, various arguments can be found in support of equality in prayer:

1. Over 50 years ago, my father[3] published an article in which he claimed, based on a historical analysis of traditional sources, that there was no partition (*mehitzah*) in synagogues of the first centuries. Although it aroused a storm of controversy in various circles at the time, both at home

---

[2] For halakhic rulings and bibliography advocating women's participation in prayer quorums, see D. Golinkin, 1992–4. "Women in the *Minyan*," in *Responsa of the Va'ad Halakhah* 5, p. 50 and n. 33 (Hebrew). See also a basic article espousing the opposite point of view: A.A. Frimer, 1986. "The Status of Women in Halakhah – Women in the *Minyan*," *Or Hamizrach* 34, pp. 69–86 (Hebrew).

[3] S. Safrai, 1963. "Was There a Women's Section in the Ancient Synagogue?" *Tarbiz* 32, pp. 329–338 (Hebrew).

and abroad, it has been reiterated in various studies over the years. Research has confirmed this claim, and it has gained acceptance in synagogue scholarship.

2. In the same article, my father also asserts that there is co-pious evidence that women were present in the synagogue. The presence of women without a partition attests to the fact that women numbered among synagogue-goers in an-cient times. This idea has resonated in other studies on the synagogue and on the role of women in the synagogue.[4]

3. I recently published,[5] together with my father, an article on the participation of women in Torah-reading in the syna-gogue, as described in the Tannaitic literature – at least during the Yavneh period. It is quite clear from the texts that the *Mishnah* and the *Tosefta* did not reject such a notion outright. In our estimation, not only was the idea not re-jected, but in the process of organizing and establishing the synagogue, following the destruction of the Temple, women became increasingly involved. If we are correct, it is inconceivable that women would not have been a part of the worshiping community, and counted for a quorum. If they are numbered among the seven (called to the Torah on the Sabbath), why would they not be counted among the ten (for a prayer quorum)? A Babylonian Talmud that

[4] S.J.D. Cohen, 1980. "The Women in the Synagogue of Antiquity," *Conservative Judaism*, 34, pp. 23–29; B. Brooten, 1982. *Women Leaders in the Ancient Synagogue*; C. Safrai, "Women and the Ancient Synagogue," in: S. Grossman & R. Haut (eds.), 1992. *Daughters of the King: Women and the Synagogue*, Philadelphia, JPS, pp. 39–49.

[5] C. Safrai & S. Safrai, 1997. "All are Called up Among the Seven," *Tarbiz* 66 (c) (1997), pp. 395–401 (Hebrew).

bars women from reading from the Torah for reasons of "public dignity," recognizes the possibility that women might do so, although they are disqualified for political reasons – which apparently were not accepted by the rabbinical authorities in the early development of the synagogue, at the time of the *Mishnah*. Our premise is that the exclusion of women from the synagogue was a socio-historical development, which occurred probably in Babylon during the Amoraic period.

4. The Jerusalem Talmud, in its commentary on *Berakhot* 5, 4, describes a situation in which all of the men in a given city are *kohanim* (members of the priestly clan). The *Gemara* asks how they can recite the Priestly Benediction without a congregation to say *amen* and receive their blessing. The answer to the question "and who will say *amen?*" is very simply "the women and children" (*ibid.* [41a]). The *Gemara* goes on to discuss whether someone standing behind or to the side of the *kohanim*, or behind a wall is able to receive the Blessing. In any case, the Jerusalem Talmud seems to indicate that women were present in the synagogue, and that they are considered a congregation, even by themselves – accompanied only by children. This is how L. Ginzburg explained this passage, astounded by the picture it presented.[6]

5. *Midrash Rabbah* on the book of Genesis seems to ascribe to Abraham consciousness of an egalitarian quorum, when he struggles to defend Sodom, and arrives at the number ten: "Why ten? because he thought that there were ten there,

---

[6] L. Ginzburg, 1961. *Commentaries and Innovations in the Yerushalmi*, New York, p. 279.

viz. Lot, his wife, his four daughters and four sons-in-law"
(*Midrash Rabbah*, Gen 49, 13; translation: *The Midrash Rabbah*, Soncino Press, London, 1977, p. 432). Ten is a minimum representative figure, and the *Midrash* includes both
women and men.

6. *Halakhic* literature cites further terms in support of the exclusion of women from public worship: *minyan* (quorum),
edah (congregation), *tzibbur* (public), and *davar shebikdushah*
(sacred matter). Apparently, women are not a part of Jewish public life when it comes to divine worship. They are
not a part of a prayer **quorum**, nor are they members of
the **congregation** when it gathers to venerate God. A Jewish **public** is a public of men, and women may not participate in any **sacred matter** that requires a quorum of men.
Here too, it would seem that each of these terms must be
examined as they appear in halakhic literature, in order to
ascertain whether in fact they cannot be seen in any way
but as requiring the exclusion of women from significant
Jewish public life.

7. Rabbis and scholars have pointed out the interesting requirement that all of Israel – men, women and children –
must be convened in order to fulfill the commandment of
hakhel (lit. "assemble" – a ceremony held every seven years
on the festival of *Sukkot*, *cf.* Deut 31:10–13 –tr.). The Rabbis, it seems, tried to construct a fundamental midrashic rationale, whereby the participation of women in covenantal
events such as the giving of the Torah at Sinai and the
commandment of *hakhel*, is seen as part of the Jewish People's social commitment to the Torah. Women thus become a part of the congregation, although the biblical
verses can be understood differently. The Rabbis preferred

to include women in covenantal obligations. There are cases in which *kahal* (assembly) or *am* (people) are understood by the Rabbis – even in sacred contexts – to include women. It is therefore incorrect to presume that the only possible reading is one that excludes women from assembly and people.

8. Such is the case with the term *edah* (congregation) as well. In the *Mishnah* (*Sanhedrin* 1, 6), the association between the word *edah* and the number ten is inferred from the case of a religious court, in which the place and role of women is a matter of dispute among halakhic authorities.[7] The *Mishnah* in *Horayot* uses *edah* in reference to those worthy of issuing legal rulings – presumably men only (*Horayot* 1:4). Similarly, the "half-shekel," which is only required of men is called "the silver of them that were numbered of the congregation (*pekudei ha'edah*)" (Ex 38:24). Nevertheless, it is worth noting that this term, as used in ancient and later literature does not necessarily exclude women. The "bullock of the congregation" serves as an atonement for all of Israel – presumably not only the men (*Tosefta, Zevahim* 10, 2). *Avot de-Rabbi Natan* (12, 4 [Schechter, p. 50]) distinguishes between *benei yisrael* ("the sons of Israel") – only the men – who wept at the death of Moses, and *kol kehal adat yisrael* ("the entire congregation of Israel") who wept at Aaron's death (Num 20:29). *Mekhilta de-Rabbi Ishmael* (*Pisha* 5 [Horowitz, p. 17]) interprets "*kol kehal adat yisrael*" as a reference to the fact that the Paschal Lamb had to be sacri-

---

[7] For halakhic rulings supporting women in judicial roles see Chief Rabbi E. Bakshi-Doron, 1979. "Authority and Leadership for Women and Converts," *Torah Shebe'al Peh* 20, pp. 66–72 (= *Responsa Binyan Av*, Section 65) (Hebrew).

ficed in three separate groups (implied by the use of three separate words: *kahal*, *edah*, and *yisrael*), making no gender distinction. It is thus clear that the word *edah* includes both men and women.

9. Maimonides (*Hilkhot Tefillah* 11, 1) asserts that any group of ten Jews is called *edah*. The word "ten" is not gender-specific *per se*, and it could include both men and women. Most such references in the works of Maimonides can be understood this way, although admittedly, at least once the term would appear to be more clearly gender-specific. In *Hilkhot Berakhot* (2, 10) Maimonides stipulates that the blessings following Grace After Meals in the presence of a newlywed couple may only be recited "in [a quorum of] ten – including the bridegroom" – making no reference to the bride. Although in Hebrew, the masculine gender includes women as well, men are more prominent. In *Hilkhot Tefillah* (8, 4), Maimonides uses the phrase "ten free [i.e., not slaves –tr.] adults," which is also not gender-specific *per se*. Although we can assume that Maimonides envisioned a group of males, his wording leaves room for a non-gender-specific point of view. Perhaps Maimonides intentionally chose such vague and inclusive language, so as not to resolve the issue one way or the other.

10. The term *davar shebikdushah* ("sacred matter") is attributed to Rabbi Ishmael, who states that all "sacred matters" require a quorum of ten. A *kohen* must be given priority in all sacred matters: to speak first, to recite the blessing first at meals, and to choose the first portion of food. The sages of the *Gemara* infer that this practice is of biblical origin, but also for reasons of social harmony (*darkei shalom*) (*Gittin* 59b *et al.*). The Babylonian sage Rabbi Ada bar Ahavah

further develops the concept and links it to sacred offices
in a quorum: "In all sacred matters there must be no fewer
than ten" (*Berakhot* 21b; *Megillah* 23b). In support of this
position, the *Gemara* cites the verse "but I will be hallowed
among the children (sons) of Israel" (Lev 22:32). It may be
the *Gemara*'s intention to interpret "the children (sons) of
Israel" as referring to men only – a common interpretation
of the term – but this is not stated explicitly. A sacred act
requires a public forum, i.e., ten people, but nowhere does
it clearly say they must be men.

11. Furthermore, none of the later commentators and halakhic
authorities restrict the concept of "ten" to a specific gender. They do in fact exclude minors and slaves (*Mahzor
Vitri* 39, 46, 278), or someone who is engaged in study at
the time of public worship (*Sefer Ha'itim* 174; *Sefer Ha'esh-
kol, Hilkhot Tefillah* 16; *Kol Bo* 8), but women are not
mentioned. In other words, there is no gender-based exclusion. This is clearly reflected in the *Arba'ah Turim* codex
(*Orah Hayim* 55) which follows Maimonides in this matter:
"The ten must be free adults [...] and some permit the
inclusion of a minor." Here too, there is no gender-based
definition. Indeed the *Tur* in *Hilkhot Birkat Hamazon* (*ibid.*
199) cites the opinion of Rabbi Yehudah Hacohen that a
woman may be counted for public recitation of Grace After Meals (*zimmun*), and the *Bayit Hadash* (*Ba"H*) comments:
"This matter can be resolved if we say that Rabbi Yehudah
only counted a woman among the ten [required] to recite
the invitation [to say Grace] with God's name, but not
among the three [required to recite the invitation itself]."
In other words, the *Ba"H* believed that a woman could be
part of a quorum of ten required to recite the invitation
with God's name. Although not numbered among the

minimum three required to recite the invitation to say Grace After Meals, she can certainly be included in a more exalted ceremony, resembling a prayer quorum. The *Beit Yosef* (Rabbi Joseph Caro) on the same passage completely rejects the possibility, remarking that it could never actually have happened – as evidenced by the fact that no one had ever seen or heard of such a thing. The exclusion of women from prayer, public recitation of Grace and Jewish communal life is a matter of debate among medieval Jewish scholars. Although tradition on the whole bars women from participating in sacred matters, there are linguistic and interpretive differences among the medieval rabbis.

The language of halakhic tradition remains vague, accommodating a reading other than the accepted one, from this point forward. There is no doubt that most halakhic authorities of the past centuries "presume" that *tzibbur*, *edah* and *kahal* are determined first and foremost by the presence of ten men. Halakhic ruling usually tends to ignore this historical process, preferring instead to consider the matter of a quorum of men to be biblically mandated (to use the words of the talmudic debate). Our interest, as noted above, lies not in the accepted process, but in examining the possibility of deviating from it, since morally, it has ceased to be accepted in western society. In fact, the language used in the traditional sources provides bold halakhists with old-new tools, and the opportunity to pour democratic wine from the flasks of Judaism and the Torah.

Socio-Religious Encounters in the Past

Appropriating the Bible:
Women and *Haskalah* in the 19th Century

TOVA COHEN

It has been a basic assumption of historical and literary research of the *Haskalah* period that, as a rule, Jewish women did not know Hebrew, and were not familiar with the canonical Hebrew texts. Many women were in fact not illiterate, and even received some level of education, but not in Hebrew. The erudition of traditional women was limited to Yiddish, while modern educated women studied European languages – German, Russian and French – exposing them to a wide variety of literature.[1] Women in general were thus left out of the cultural-literary revolution going on at the time, and are generally believed to have appeared on the Hebrew intellectual and literary scene only in the early 20th century.[2]

Some of the creative figures of the day, particularly toward the end of the *Haskalah* period, took note of this fact. The poet J.L.

---

[1] For a specific breakdown of the languages studied by 19th century women, see I. Parush, 2001. *Reading Women: The Benefit of Marginality in Nineteenth Century Eastern European Jewish Society*, Am Oved, Tel Aviv (Hebrew).

[2] This is, for example, the basic assumption of D. Meron, 1991. *Founding Mothers, Stepsisters, On Two Beginnings of Modern Poetry in the Land of Israel*, Hakibbutz Hameuhad (Hebrew).

Gordon for example, in his poem *"Le-Mi Ani Amel"* ("For Whom Do I Toil") (1871), bemoans the fact that there were no women among his readers, as they were forbidden to study Hebrew, the "Holy Tongue":

> **Sisters, daughters of Zion!**
> **You may give heed to my verse,**
> **And God has given you charming souls,**
> **Graceful spirits, discerning tastes, and warm hearts within –**
> **But alas, you have been raised in captivity,**
> **For "a daughter taught Torah – has lechery gained!"**[3]

A generation later, H.N. Bialik still describes women's ignorance of Hebrew language and literature:

> The iniquity [...] is, that only males were educated. **Half the nation remained without any education**. [...] This was a criminal offense and a dangerous tragedy. If the gentile women were an obstacle in the days of Ezra and Nehemiah, **our own women have become gentile women**, and an obstacle to the education of our children [emphasis mine].[4]

I will not elaborate here on the reasons why women were excluded from study and the Hebrew language in traditional Jewish society. Suffice it to note that the forced ignorance of women in the language of high culture and canonical literature is not unique to Jewish society, but is typical of patriarchal societies, in which

---

[3] J.L. Gordon, 1959. *Works; Poetry*, Dvir, Tel-Aviv, p. 27 (Hebrew).

[4] H.N. Bialik, 1935. *Devarim Shebe'al Peh*, vol. 1, Dvir, Tel-Aviv, p. 26 (Hebrew).

women are thus "silenced."[5] The exclusion of women from the canonical culture and its language (Hebrew) was further supported in traditional Jewish society by the religious injunction against women studying Torah.[6]

One might have expected a conscious and intentional change in this matter, on the part of the Hebrew *Haskalah* movement, spearhead of an ideological, cultural and linguistic revolution that began in the late 18th century. The *Haskalah* movement however, which openly challenged central elements of Jewish society (clericalism; lack of productivity; ignorance of general culture), made virtually no attempt to change the status of women. A number of writers indeed paid lip service to the issue,[7] but in effect continued to accept – consciously or unconsciously – the traditional position, whereby intellectual pursuits and high culture were restricted to men. *Haskalah* literature was seen by its creators and readers as "men's literature" – for members of the "club."

Nevertheless, beginning in the mid-nineteenth century, at the height of the *Haskalah* period, the single-gender nature of *Haskalah* literature began to change, when **women began to learn Hebrew, to read Hebrew *Haskalah* literature and even to write in Hebrew**. It was a thin stream, almost subterranean, but the number of women writers began to grow in the '70s and '80s, finally

---

[5] See for example, J. Donoven, 1980. "The Silence is Broken," in S. McConnell-Ginet, R. Borker and N. Furmar (eds.), *Women and Language in Literature and Society*, Praeger, New York, pp. 205–218.

[6] For a detailed list of sources and rulings on women studying Torah, see E.G. Elinson, 1974. *Ha'ishah Vehamitzvot*, Jerusalem (Hebrew).

[7] See my article "What Have I to Do with A Wise Woman: The Literary Formulation of the Hebrew *Maskilah* from Various Gender-Related Perspectives," in J. Bar-el et al. (eds.), 2000. *Literature and Society in Modern Hebrew Culture: Papers in Honor of Gershon Shaked*, Hakibbutz Hameuchad (Hebrew), pp. 38–61.

emerging in the early 20th century, in the stories of women authors of the First Aliyah[8] and Deborah Baron; and in the poetry of Rahel, Esther Raab, Elisheva and Yocheved Bat-Miriam.

A study presently underway, has discovered the Hebrew works of over 20 women who saw themselves as part of the *Haskalah* movement.[9] These writings were found in manuscript archives as well as publications of the period. A number of these women writers were known among contemporary *maskilim* (women such as Miriam Markel-Mosessohn, who corresponded in Hebrew with many famous *maskilim*, or Rachel Morpurgo, whose poems were published in the *Haskalah* periodical, *Kokhvei Yitzhak*). Others however, never published their works, or – even if they did – went unnoticed. The *maskilim* themselves, as well as researchers of the period, although familiar perhaps with a few of these women, saw them merely as curiosities.

Conversely, the works themselves, viewed as a body and in light of the development of women's writing in Hebrew, present **these Hebrew *maskilot* as the forerunners of change in the place of women within the new Hebrew intellectual world.** Although each of them felt isolated in her work and aspirations, they were all part of a wider phenomenon of women who had acquired Hebrew education and tried to penetrate the closed male world of *Haskalah* literature. These *maskilot* did not wait for He-

---

[8] For example, N. Pukhachewsky, H. Ben-Yehudah and H. Trager. A selection of their stories can be found in: Y. Berlovitz, 1984. *Stories of Women of the First Aliya*, Tarmil, Misrad Habitachon Press, Tel Aviv (Hebrew). For English language studies in this field, see: C.B. Balin, 2000. *To Reveal Our Hearts: Jewish Women Writers in Tsarist Russia*, Hebrew Union College, Cincinnati; W. Zierler, "The Rabbi's Daughter In and Out of the Kitchen: Feminist Literary Negotiations," *Nashim* 5 (2002), pp. 83–104.

[9] I am conducting the study at Bar-Ilan University, together with Prof. Shmuel Feiner.

brew to become a spoken language. They studied Hebrew, despite its being the language of male culture (what anthropologist Walter Ong has termed the "father tongue" – high language used to convey the canonical culture, and acquired in educational institutions, as opposed to the "mother tongue," the language of everyday speech, learned at home[10]). Studying Hebrew, reading its literature, and writing in that language, indicate a conscious effort on the part of women to cross the high gender barrier that lay between women and the Hebrew language.

Moreover, many women students of Hebrew did not stop at the mechanical acquisition of vocabulary and grammar, but also sought to master parts of the canonical literature (primarily, but not exclusively, the Bible), consequently enriching their writing with references to these works. Writing in high language, incorporating nuances of meaning from the canonical religious texts, was a central prerequisite of *Haskalah* literature, and of the subsequent literature of national rebirth. Some of the women were quite successful in this: **Not only were they familiar with the canonical sources and able to weave them into their writing, but they also appropriated the texts, adding a new personal-feminine dimension to them**. The appropriation of sacred and canonical texts, adapting their meaning to feminine expression, is typical of women's writing in general,[11] and of modern Hebrew women's writing as well.[12] We will try to prove that this phenomenon is not only a characteristic of modern Hebrew women's

[10] W. J. Ong, 1981. *Fighting for Life*, Cornell Univ. Press, Ithaca-London.

[11] A. Ostriker, 1985. "The Thieves of Language," in E. Showalter (ed.), *The New Feminist Criticism*, Pantheon Books, New York, pp. 314–338.

[12] See for example, L. Rattok, 1996. "Like Hewing Water; Motifs in Women's Hebrew Poetry," in Z. Shamir (ed.), *Studies in Hebrew Literature*, Tel-Aviv University, pp. 165–202 (Hebrew).

writing, but **began with the appropriation of canonical Hebrew texts in the works of 19th century Hebrew *maskilot*.**

Examples of the appropriation of canonical texts can be found in many of the works collected. To illustrate, we have chosen passages from three different genres: a poem ("Woe, My Soul Will Say," by Rachel Morpurgo, 1847);[13] a letter (by Miriam Markel-Mosessohn, 1863);[14] and an essay ("The Question of Women," by Toybe Segal, 1879).[15]

The three excerpts have a common theme: the authors all address a woman's desire to study, and her frustration at the negative attitude of Jewish – and even *Haskalah* – society, toward this aspiration. The figure presented in the texts is that of an intellectual woman, seeking a mode of expression and self-fulfillment specifically in the Hebrew language and the field of Jewish canonical lore, while being fully aware of the contrast between prevailing opinions about women and her own sincere goal of acquiring education and independence, as well as her proven ability as a Hebrew writer. Thus for example, Rachel Morpurgo claims that due to negative attitudes regarding the intellectual capabilities of women, her poetry would be forgotten by all who now praise her. She ends her poem with an ironic reference to prevailing opinion: "The witness will attest, seated or walking about\ there is no wisdom among women, but at the distaff." Miriam Markel-Mosessohn describes the very same situation, openly admitting her fear of being shunned by society for venturing into a "forbidden field": "They will call

---

[13] From R. Morpurgo, 1890. *Ugav Rahel*, Cracow, p. 54 (Hebrew).

[14] Letter to Rabbi Landsberg (July 1863), Jewish National and University Library, Schwadron Collection, autograph no. 77455 (Hebrew).

[15] The essay was published in several parts in *Ha-Ivri* (1880), pp. 69; 77–78; 85; 94; 101–102 (Hebrew). It was first mentioned in S. Feiner's article, "The Modern Jewish Woman: A Test-Case in the Relationship between *Haskalah* and Modernity," *Zion* 98 (1993), pp. 453–499 (Hebrew).

after me […] behold a maid whose fathers have taught her Torah, it is an iniquity."

The most poignant description of this state of affairs is that of Toybe Segal, whose long essay is devoted to criticism of male-Jewish society's treatment of women, and the importance of education for girls. The essay's ironic tone and portrayal of the painful contrast between truth and convention, are established in the opening paragraph:

> I am a Hebrew maid, and in Hebrew I will speak my heart, for it is my whole life. And although I know that the question of women will not be resolved in the Hebrew periodicals, and certainly not by **me**, a **frivolous** woman[…] I will gather my strength, and **like a man** gird up my loins to wage with my poor pen, the war of **women**.[16] [emphasis in original]

Beyond the thematic common denominators between the women authors, a common morphological style developed, despite predominant differences between the different genres: **The demand for women's education is strengthened on a cultural-linguistic level: All of the women authors have a good command of the canonical sources, which they apply to their revolutionary writing**. In this very ability, they undermine the rationale of those who would silence them, of the perception embodied in expressions such as: "He who teaches his daughter Torah, it is as if he has taught her lechery," or "women are frivolous."

We will now demonstrate the appropriation of canonical sources through specific analysis of examples from the texts we have chosen to address. It can perhaps be claimed that the use of

---

[16] *Ibid.*, p. 69.

biblical references is an integral part of *Haskalah* Hebrew, which is high literary language, and as such does not always impart a new meaning to the texts. Indeed, even if the women authors "only" employed biblical language in a lexical fashion, this proves their fluency in the "father tongue" – the language of canonical culture considered the province of men. We will try to prove however that the women writers use biblical references, knowing the original contexts and employing these contexts to give meaning to their own writing, often through a new and different woman's reading of the canonical text.

Due to the length of the prose works, we will only cite selected passages. We will however present Rachel Morpurgo's entire poem, which is relatively short, to ensure better comprehension.

First Example: Letter from Miriam Markel-Mosessohn to Rabbi H. Landsberg, July 1863

The letter is a reply to Rabbi Landsberg's letter, written in praise of an article of hers published in *Hamaggid*. In the letter, she describes how she acquired her education with her parents' encouragement in her youth, how she began to study Hebrew and how she began to write in Hebrew, despite the fact that this was not acceptable behavior for a woman:

> For who shall notice whether an innocent young maid acquires knowledge or not? And who cares if my soul has become a little refined with the tenderness and delicacy of the sweet singers of Israel. I have **greatly feared** at times that my meager knowledge might be **wanting**, that a **multitude** might **call after me**, behold a maid, whose fathers have taught her Torah, it is **an iniquity that were sin**. And only **this was my comfort**, when **my heart was in-**

132

diting a matter or **my thoughts** awakened **within me**, that you have always put ink on paper and in that I have found **delight**, but never had I imagined that the fruit of my poor pen would please a sophisticated palate. [emphasis mine]

The language, as in all of Markel-Mosenssohn's letters, is replete with biblical words and expressions (some of which I have emphasized in the above excerpt). She does not however, merely shape and personalize the biblical vocabulary. She carefully selects her words from contexts that imbue her thoughts with deeper meaning.

The references in the first part of the passage systematically evoke verses pertaining to fear of the reactions of others, guilt and a lack of faith in one's environment. The verses that are thus drawn into the letter, deepen the expression of the author's fears that arose from her having dared to study Hebrew, and indirectly strengthen her criticism of the society that had made her feel guilty:

"For the thing which I **greatly feared** is come upon me" (Job 3:25).
"That which is crooked cannot be made straight: and that which is **wanting** cannot be numbered" (Ecc 1:15).
"For even thy brethren and the house of thy father…, yea they **have called a multitude after thee**: believe them not, though they speak fair words unto thee" (Jer 12:6).
"In all my labors they shall find none **iniquity in me that were sin**" (Hos 12:9).

The biblical references in the second part of the passage are no less significant. The three main verses cited are from the book of Psalms, and all pertain to the sense of comfort the biblical speaker derives from his connection with God:

"**This is my comfort** in my affliction: for thy word hath quickened me" (Ps 119:50).
"**My heart is inditing a** good **matter**: I speak of the things I have made touching the king: my tongue is the pen of a ready writer" (*ibid.* 45:2).
"In the multitude of **my thoughts within me** thy comforts **delight** my soul" (*ibid.* 94:19).

The second verse clearly attests to the author's intentions in selecting the context of the references as complementing the modern text. She describes her feelings in general terms: "my heart was inditing a matter." The second part of the verse however, expresses what she has not said explicitly: "the pen of a ready writer." Moreover, **the author reverses the original meaning of the verses** on two levels: The first level is quite common in *Haskalah* writing – presenting the literary work as the modern heir to the religious expression of the biblical speaker: the comforts that delight the soul of the author derive from her creative ability, not her relationship with God. This type of secularization of the biblical verse is typical of a number of prominent poets of the *Haskalah*, who portray themselves as prayer-leaders or modern-day prophets – who present their own gospel rather than that of God.[17]

The second level – that of appropriation of the verse – is apparent from the very fact that the verses of the biblical poet have been adopted, in the first person. Not only does the author count herself among the readers of Hebrew poetry ("my soul has become a little refined with the tenderness and delicacy of the sweet singers

---

[17] For further details and examples see my article "From Prayer-leader to Prophet – The Evolution of Prayers and Prophecies in *Haskalah* Poetry," *Bar-Ilan Year Book*, 24–25 (1989), pp. 61–82 (Hebrew).

of Israel"), but from the fact that she does not hesitate to apply the expressions of the Psalmist to herself, she affords legitimacy to a woman's writing in Hebrew – an action ascribed in the biblical original to men only.

Appropriation of the biblical expressions is thus not only a linguistic technique which Miriam Markel-Mosessohn employs masterfully; but like the best *Haskalah* writers, through the biblical verse gives added meaning to her writing, even daring to intimate gender insights contrary to those of her society and time.

Second Example: Toybe Segal, "The Question of Women"

In this feminist essay, Toybe Segal describes the status of women in the entire range of Jewish society – from the most conservative circles to the most enlightened. In all of these, she claims, women suffer discrimination, because they are denied the chance to study, which would enable them to develop as equal human beings. Her feminist views were undoubtedly influenced by revolutionary Russian feminism of the day, which also touted women's education as the most important basis for women's equality at home and in society.[18]

Like other *maskilim*, Toybe Segal's language is filled with biblical expressions. In the opening of her essay however, she employs another method of biblical citation: She relates to a specific biblical image, interpreting it in a traditional manner, and then portrays the present as a new and different variation of that image. At the beginning of the essay, she introduces a verse from Isaiah (4:1) as a motto: "And in that day seven women shall take hold of one man,

---

[18] On the Russian feminist struggle for equality in education as a basis for women's independence and equality in society and the family, see R. Sites, 1978. *The Women's Liberation Movement in Russia*, Princeton Univ. Press.

saying, We will eat our own bread, and wear our own apparel: only let us be called by thy name, to take away our reproach." Introducing a biblical verse as a motto, a common practice in *Haskalah* literature, lends added validity to the new text. The verse cited here however, does not serve as a classic motto, but rather as a point of departure for a bitter and ironic description of the status of women who are dependent upon men. Immediately following the opening paragraph, in which she describes the aim of her essay – "Perhaps my words will find their way into the hearts of some readers, causing them to change their views on the state of their daughters' education" – she goes on to interpret the scene described in the motto. First, she explains it in a traditional, historical fashion, demonstrating her biblical erudition:

> The days in which the son of Amoz described his terrible vision of matters that go down into the innermost parts of the belly [...] matters concerning the captivity of the daughters of Zion and its young men, to forewarn them, that days of battle will approach, and that Zion, our beloved city, would remain as a lodge in a garden of watermelons [...] and there would be no shelter for its maidens, and no one to take away their reproach on the day of trouble [...] on which seven women shall take hold of one man, beseeching him to extend his protection to them, letting them be called by his name, that they might not be naked unto their shame.

She doesn't stop there however. She then turns the biblical scene into a metaphor of the state of women in her time:

> For even in these days of freedom and liberty, the daughters of Jacob do not know the judgments of liberty[...] And the difference between the days of the son of Amoz and the present is only this: For then[...] very few inclined their ears to

hear his words[…] while today statistics have become a lying spirit in the mouths of many[…] who cry[…]: Look and behold the statistics that women are sevenfold the number of men in the world, and the value of men is therefore very dear[…] and the value of women has come down wonderfully.

The author presents the historical description of seven women taking hold of one man, as a result of a war in which most of the men had been killed, in order to compare the situation to that of her own time, in which women were in the same humiliating position. The present humiliation however, is not the result of tragic social circumstances (as in the past), but rather the consequence of an inegalitarian chauvinistic way of thinking. It was apparently common practice in her time to use statistics (false statistics in her opinion), stating that the number of women in the world was much higher than the number of men, to urge women to hold on to any man that comes along. This is her interpretation of "seven women shall take hold of one man," and it reflects an even more humiliating situation than the one described in the Bible. The historical scene portrayed in the biblical verse is used by the author for the sake of comparison to her own time, the necessary conclusion being that despite significant progress in all aspects of life, attitudes to women had not changed, and had perhaps even worsened.

On another level, the very discussion of this biblical passage by a woman writer is further proof of the absurdity of the chauvinist premise that lies at the heart of the entire essay: that women are not capable, and should not study.

Third Example: Rachel Morpurgo, "Woe, My Soul Will Say"

Woe, my soul will say, bitterly bitter
My spirit struck me and I was haughty
I heard a voice say: Your poetry is preserved
Who compares to thee, Rachel who studies song?
My spirit will reply: My scent is changed
Exile upon exile, my skin stiffened
My taste gone, my vineyard pruned
I fear disgrace I will sing no more.

I will turn to the north south east and west
A woman's mind is frivolous, for that she is raised.
A few years later, why now –

Should a dead dog be remembered in every town and province?
The witness will attest, seated or walking about
There is no wisdom among women, but at the distaff.

I have analyzed this poem in detail elsewhere, [19] demonstrating that Morpurgo appropriates canonical texts from different periods. Morpurgo apparently possessed vast knowledge of Jewish sources – most unusual for a woman of her time. She studied not only Bible, but also Talmud and Kabbalah as well, and would seem to have been familiar with a great many *piyyutim*, through her

---

[19] T. Cohen, 1996. "Inside and Outside Culture: On the Appropriation of the 'Father Tongue' as a Path to the Intellectual Development of Women's Self-Image," in *Studies in Hebrew Literature*, Tel-Aviv University, pp. 69–110 (Hebrew).

cousin, S.D. Luzzatto, who was a great collector of *piyyutim*.[20] She therefore, unlike other women of her time, was able to call upon a very wide variety of Jewish sources. Thus for example, the entire poem reads like a feminine echo of Solomon Ibn Gabirol's "*Shelishit Shokedet Meshaleshet Tzevaha.*"[21] Clear linguistic ties refer the reader to this *piyyut* (unusual words and expressions appearing in Morpurgo's poem are intentional references to it: "*samar*" {"stiffened"}, "*mar li mar*" {"bitterly bitter"}, "*etyamar*" {"I am haughty"}, "*reihi namar*" {"my scent is changed"}). While Ibn Gabirol uses the image of a suffering woman as a metaphor for the Jewish People awaiting divine redemption ("Will I be forever cast in exile\ Has God forgotten my pleas"), Morpurgo returns the description to its original image – that of the suffering woman.

Other sources used by Morpurgo are talmudic. In describing the pride she should feel at the publication of her poetry, Morpurgo writes: "My spirit struck me and I was haughty" – based on a description of male pride in the Talmud: "They made me a broad stage and seated me upon it, and my spirit struck me" (JT *Yevamot* 12, 6). Unlike the talmudic protagonist however, the speaker in Morpurgo's poem feels sorrow rather than pride: "Woe, my soul will say, bitterly bitter," knowing that because she was a woman, her poetry would soon be forgotten. Other talmudic sources are also quoted in a sense that runs contrary to their original meaning. In the final two stanzas she cites well-known talmudic adages: "A woman's mind is frivolous" (*Shabbat* 33b); "There is no wisdom among women, but at the distaff" (*Yoma* 66b). These adages stand in contradiction to the praise lavished upon Morpurgo by various writers, but it is in the talmudic sayings that she identifies male

---

[20] See introduction by H.Y. Castiglioni ("Life of the Poetess") to *Ugav Rahel*, Cracow, 1890 (Hebrew).

[21] See D. Yarden 1977. *The Sacred Poetry of Rabbi Solomon Ibn Gabirol*, vol. 1, Jerusalem, pp. 303–304 (Hebrew).

society's true opinion of women, and in so doing, her criticism of it is implied.

Among the wealth of Jewish sources cited by Morpurgo, there is also a biblical verse (Jer 48:11), appearing in the second stanza, adding gender-related meaning to the poem:

> My spirit will reply: **My scent is changed**
> **Exile upon exile**, my skin stiffened
> **My taste gone**, my vineyard pruned,
> I fear disgrace I will sing no more. [all emphasis mine]

The verse in Jeremiah 48:11 reads:

> Moab hath been at ease from his youth, and he hath settled on his lees, and hath not been emptied from vessel to vessel, **neither hath he gone into exile: therefore his taste remained in him, and his scent is not changed.**

The poet's intention, in comparing the verse to the poem, placing them side by side, is to explain her sense of failure. The subject described in the poem is the exact opposite of the one in the biblical verse. The subject of Jeremiah's description maintains his vitality over time, while the subject in the poem immediately loses her vitality and taste ("her scent is changed"), following "exile upon exile."

The verse indeed explicitly states that it is referring to Moab, but the description in the masculine, as opposed to the feminine speaker in the poem, makes the contrast gender-related as well: the man, quiet and at ease, achieves success, while a woman never attains ease, and thus never achieves success either. To this basic existential state she adds the fact that she has not succeeded in writing as she would have liked: "I fear disgrace I will sing no more." This line, which rhymes (in Hebrew) with the last line of the previous stanza ("Who compares to thee, Rachel who studies song"), links the two stanzas: The speaker refuses to enjoy the praises of society (first stanza) because her work is not worthy of such praise. As a woman, she lacks the ease and confidence necessary for artistic creation (second stanza).

* * *

The three examples we have brought represent an unknown phenomenon in the development of Hebrew *Haskalah* culture in the 19th century. Not only were there women who studied, read and wrote Hebrew during the *Haskalah* period, thus crossing the linguistic-cultural divide between men and women, but a few of these women even tried to penetrate the world of canonical male textual knowledge. Their writings reflect this ability in their very use of the biblical vocabulary, and in the way in which they add further meaning to their texts through biblical references. These educated women appropriate the canonical texts and adapt them to the women's perspectives, often subversive, that they wish to express. I believe these early women Hebrew writers should be seen as the forerunners of modern Hebrew women's writing, and their ability to appropriate canonical texts as the beginning of modern women's Jewish scholarship.

Written by Men for Men: Feminist Revolution and Innovation in the Canonical Sources

NAFTALI ROTHENBERG

1. Introduction

Jewish canonical literature was written by men. In that, it is no different from all classical cultural works, created over thousands of years, within cultural and social contexts that discriminated against women and excluded them from public circles. The exclusion of women from the field of literature was absolute – not because women did not write, in any case only a few writers ever participate in literary discourse, but also because they did not read. In other words, women in general had no connection to literature; its writers and readers were all men. The books of the Bible, the *Mishnah*, the Talmuds, *Midrash*, Gaonic literature, medieval Jewish philosophy, *Kabbalah* literature and the *Zohar*, were all written by men for men.

This fact, which is the product of particular social and cultural circumstances, must be recognized by those who seek to reveal the "feminine voice" in the traditional sources, and by those who would discover the truth regarding the slow development of the status of women over the generations. Accepting the fact that women were excluded from the world of literary creation and consumption, and even the attempt to understand the socio-cultural environment that brought about this fact, are not enough. The important question is whether the men who produced literature took this reality for granted, or strove to change it? Was their position on the status of women in keeping with the gender reality of their time, or did it differ? Did the male writers dare to offer new interpretations? Did they have a message to convey to their contemporaries, or did they merely reflect contemporary culture?

As noted above, these important questions pertain to human culture in general. This article only addresses Jewish canonical sources. As an example – one of many – of the universality of this discussion however, one could cite Sophocles' *Antigone*. This play, written in the fifth century B.C. by a man and for men (who also performed the women's roles) raises the problem of the status of women at the time, in all its intensity. As such, it conveys a message to the contemporary culture, and does not merely make due with reflecting it. Antigone was ahead of her time, as a woman who had the ability to choose freely, and who accepted the moral imperative on an equal level, without hiding behind a man or in the shadow of a man's authority, even if that man was the king. She pays with her life for having been ahead of her time. The real tragedy in this play however, does not lie in her death but rather in the ruin of the king, whose order she disobeyed of her own free will, in order to uphold the moral imperative. In effect, Antigone afforded the king another chance to obey the moral code. In rejecting this code, he brought destruction upon himself, under-mining society as a whole. The feminine voice in the play, that of Antigone, is a heroic one, and Sophocles – the man who wrote for men – can therefore be said to have given expression to feminist innovation in his play.

The attempt to describe and document feminist innovation and revolution in Jewish sources may be misleading inasmuch as it presents an idyllic picture that inadequately expresses a discriminatory socio-cultural reality, and the prevailing views among the men who wrote these works. It is important to emphasize that the terms "innovation" and "revolution" merely refer to positions that diverge from the prevailing social and cultural norm. The idyllic picture that may arise from the fact that this article focuses on innovation within the traditional sources, is not presented intentionally in order to describe a non-existent reality. Nevertheless, we must guard against the widespread tendency toward anachronistic judgment of views expressed in traditional texts. Any judgment of the positions taken by these writers and thinkers must be done within the context of the socio-cultural reality within which they lived. We must not impose upon them the values and concepts of our own culture. The force of feminist innovation and revolution in the canonical sources is measured in relation to the cultural surroundings and values of the society in which these works were created.

2. A Monogamous Message to a Polygamous Culture

Polygamy, practiced to this day in various parts of the world, was the accepted social norm throughout all of the periods in which Jewish canonical literature was created. The Bible itself tells us of polygamy in biblical times, but again, this was the prevailing practice throughout the world, practically up to the modern era. Having many wives was an expression of wealth and social status – meaning that women who were their husbands' only wives were not necessarily better off. The culture of marriage between a single man and a number of women – and among the aristocracy, princes and kings, a single man and many women – was deeply ingrained in the common identity, among men and women alike. Polygamy declined however, in those areas that came under Christian influence, despite the fact that the vast majority of Christian converts –

both willing and unwilling – hailed from the lower classes, and thus could not afford more than one wife anyway. This was especially true of Europe. Later, European-Christian imperialism attempted – not always successfully – to impose monogamy upon the cultures it conquered in the west and the east. European-Christian influence often persisted long after the liberation of Muslim and far-eastern countries from European rule. In some Muslim countries, polygamy has only recently been outlawed, as a result of democratization and policies aimed at limiting population growth, while some Muslim countries still allow men to marry a number of women. In eastern cultures, polygamy continued into the 20th century, and only the erosion of traditional culture, particularly under communist regimes, reduced its prevalence.

If this was the case in polygamous societies 1,000–2,000 years after the biblical era, how much more so at the time of the Bible: 3,500 and more years ago. During these periods, monogamous concepts were foreign to the prevailing culture and identity, as if from another world, and their appearance in the Pentateuch is a veritable revolution – the beginning of a revolution adopted by most of the world thousands of years later – which made little headway when it first began, even in later biblical times.

In the Bible, we find ample evidence of polygamy. At the very beginning of the book of Genesis, the Bible tells us about the first bigamist: "And Lamech took unto him two wives: the name of the one was Adah, and the name of the other Zillah" (Gen 4:19). The commentators and midrashists saw in Lamech's action the beginning of a flaw in human behavior. The practice spread and was adopted by many, and was one of the expressions of the decadence of the generation of the flood. The commentators suggest that many men at the time would marry one wife for procreation, and another solely for the sake of sexual pleasure. The latter would drink a certain liquid that would induce sterility, in order to prevent her from becoming pregnant. Lamech did not do so, or at least he was not successful in inducing sterility in one of his wives, because the Torah emphasizes that both bore children: "And Adah bare Jabal: he was the father of all such as dwell in tents, and of such as have cattle. And his brother's name was Jubal: he was the father of all such as handle the harp and organ. And Zillah **she also** bare Tubal-cain, an instructor of every artificer in brass and iron: and the sister of Tubal-cain was Naamah" (Gen 5:20–22). Contrary to expectations or common practice, "Zillah **she also** bare." The very fact that the two women are even mentioned is unusual, since the Bible usually lists only fathers and sons in its accounts of the generations, and women are not mentioned at all – as if having no status in the births of their children.

Later, the Bible tells of Abraham, who is prompted by his wife Sarah to take her handmaiden Hagar as a wife, and she gives birth to Ishmael. According to the plain meaning of the text, Abraham also had a third wife: "Then again Abraham took a wife, and her name was Keturah" (Gen 25:1), whom he married following the death of Sarah. The Midrash tells us that Keturah was in fact Hagar, whom Abraham had reinstated – possibly supported by the account in 1 Chronicles: "Now the sons of Keturah, Abraham's **concubine**: she bare Zimran and Jokshan ..." (I Chron 1:32).

The authors tell us of Esau's three wives. The first two were Canaanite women (Gen 26:34), "which were a grief of mind unto Isaac and to Rebekah"; and the third, whom he married in order to satisfy his parents, was his cousin Mahlath, the daughter of Ishmael (Gen 28:8). His brother Jacob intends to marry Rachel, his beloved (*ibid.* 29:18–28), but is tricked by her father: "And it came to pass, that in the morning, behold, it was Leah." Jacob does not give up on Rachel, and marries her as well. His two wives later present him with two concubines – Zilpah and Bilhah (ibid. 30:1–5) – and together, the four women give birth to the tribes of Israel.

Despite the biblical injunction against a king of Israel marrying many wives (Deut 17:17), the phenomenon of polygamy is particularly evident among the kings. David marries Abigail, wife of Nabal the Carmelite, and Ahinoam the Jezreelite (I Sam 25:39–44), as well as other women, wives and concubines (II Sam 5:13) and of course Bathsheba (*ibid.* 11:27).

The prime example of polygamous culture in the time of the Bible was King Solomon, who submitted to no restriction on the number of women or their nationality, and took hundreds of wives and concubines, including many foreign women: "But king Solomon loved many strange women, together with the daughter of Pharaoh, women of the Moabites, Edomites, Zidonians, and Hittites; Of the nations concerning which the Lord said unto the children of Israel, Ye shall not go in to them, neither shall they come in unto you: for surely they will turn away your heart after their gods: Solomon clave unto these in love. And he had seven hundred wives, princesses, and three hundred concubines: and his wives turned away his heart" (I Kings 11:1–3). His wisdom did not prevail in this case, and the Bible criticizes him for it, noting that his foreign wives turned his heart after other gods.

Rehoboam, King of Judah after Solomon, had 18 wives and 60 concubines (II Chron 11:21). Abijah, who ruled after Rehoboam, had 14 wives (*ibid.* 13:21). Further passages attest to polygamy among wealthy men and judges, including Elkanah, the father of Samuel, who had 2 wives (I Sam 1), and Gideon, whose many wives gave him 70 sons (Jud 8:30).

All of these accounts illustrate the well-known fact that the various cultures of the biblical period were polygamous. Any discussion of messages dating from this period regarding relations between the sexes and the status of women, must therefore take this into consideration.

Biblical accounts of polygamy, as an immanent part of the culture of the day, include criticism, sometimes intimated and at other times explicit, of the phenomenon itself. We have already mentioned the figure of Lamech, the first bigamist, who does not appear in a positive light. The fact that he had taken two wives is not sanctioned, although not explicitly condemned. The phenomenon that began with Lamech proliferated, as suggested perhaps by the following verses: "And it came to pass, when man began to multiply on the face of the earth, and daughters were born unto them, That the sons of God saw the daughters of men that they were fair; and they took them wives of all which they chose. And the Lord said, My spirit shall not always strive with man, for that he is also flesh: yet his days shall be a hundred and twenty years" (Gen 6:1–3). These verses are considered to be rather enigmatic, but one might take them to mean that "the sons of God," i.e., the sons of the rich and powerful were not satisfied with taking a single wife, as did most of their ancestors. The first man had one wife, and this was the practice, until the time of Lamech, as noted above. When the population increased however ("when men began to multiply"), those who could afford to do so, socially and economically, "took them wives of all which they chose," without any moral qualms. The Bible sharply criticizes the phenomenon, which, according to the plain meaning of the text, might be considered one of the causes of the terrible punishment that was the flood.

The language used by the Bible to describe the increase in population is interesting: In Genesis 1 ("Let us make *Adam* in our image, after our likeness: and let **them** have dominion …"), the word *Adam* appears first in the singular, but is later treated as plural: "when *Adam* began to multiply … and daughters were born unto **them**." This further supports the version appearing in chapter 5: "Male and female created he them; and he blessed them, and called their name *Adam*," i.e., the name *Adam* ("man") is common to both male and female, indicating a state of wholeness when they are together.

The taking of many wives by the rich and powerful was thus an immoral act, an expression of corruption, and numbered among the causes of the flood. It is therefore clear that in the process of saving creation, through Noah and the ark built by God's command, the message of monogamy is emphasized. The Bible tells us that Noah went into the ark with **his wife**, his sons, and **their wives**. The idea of pairs however does not end there. In response to human corruption, the animals, pure and impure, will also come into the ark in pairs of male and female. There is no doubt that the overemphasis on couples and pairs in the flood story strives to establish the idea as a moral standard for all mankind.

It would thus appear that the Bible does not merely criticize polygamy, but expresses a clear preference for monogamy. Despite repeated accounts of polygamous relationships – reflecting sociocultural reality – it has been quite evident to readers throughout the ages that the Bible prefers relationships comprising one man and one woman. This biblical message concerning relationships is highlighted by the prevailing polygamous culture of the time.

This unique biblical view appears at the very moment man first sets foot on the earth: "And God said, Let us make *Adam* in our image, after our likeness: and let them [in plural! and according to the next verse, it is clear why – there are two, man and woman] have dominion over the fish of the sea, and over the fowl of the air[...] So God created *Adam* in his own image, in the image of God created he him; male and female created he them. And God blessed them, and God said unto them, Be fruitful, and multiply, and replenish the earth, and subdue it" (Gen 1:26–28).

According to the simple meaning of the passage, the creation of *Adam* "in our image, after our likeness" included both male and female. Following creation, the word "*Adam*" came to refer only to the male, although at the time of creation the concept comprised both sexes, and appears as a designation for both male and female together: "This is the book of the generations of Adam. In the day that God created man, in the likeness of God made he him; Male and female created he them; and blessed them, and called their name Adam, in the day when they were created" (Gen 5:1–2).

"God's image" is manifested in their creation as male and female, together constituting the image of God in the world. "Adam" is the joint name of the first couple, in whose creation God imprinted the model of monogamy for all generations to come.

The story of man's creation appears three times in Genesis. In the account of the six days of creation, there are three verses pertaining to man's creation on the sixth day, in which we are told that man was created male and female in God's image. In chapter 5, the Torah repeats the story in two verses, again noting that man was created male and female in God's image. In between these two passages however, there is a third passage, which appears to differ significantly from the other two. The plain meaning of the story told in Genesis 2 is that at first man was created male alone, and only afterward was woman fashioned from his rib – neither creation in God's image, nor equal creation of male and female: "And the Lord God formed *Adam* of the dust of the ground, and breathed into his nostrils the breath of life; and *Adam* became a living soul. … And the Lord God said, It is not good that *Adam* should be alone; I will make him an help meet for him. … And the Lord God caused a deep sleep to fall upon Adam, and he slept: and he took one of his ribs, and closed up the flesh instead thereof. And the rib, which the Lord God had taken from *Adam*, made he a woman, and brought her unto *Adam*. And Adam said, This is now bone of my bones, and flesh of my flesh: she shall be called Woman, because she was taken out of Man. Therefore shall a man leave his father and his mother, and shall cleave unto his wife: and they shall be one flesh" (Gen. 2:7, 18, 21–24).

The plain meaning of these verses is not consistent with the egalitarian version of *Adam*'s male and female creation, as told in chapter 1 and chapter 5. It leaves little room however, for polygamy. On the contrary, it carries a strong message in support of monogamous relationships. One woman was created from a rib taken from one man, and for her sake he will leave his father and

Feminist Revolution and Innovation

his mother and cleave unto her and they will be one flesh. Leaving his father and his mother who gave him life and raised him to adulthood, cleaving to his wife and the unity of flesh, are raised here to the level of the purpose of mankind's existence. Paradoxically, man on his own, as an individual, is not united and harmonious within himself, but rather alone and isolated. Unity is manifested through cleaving to a single partner, who is bone of his bones, flesh of his flesh, taken from him, and without whom he is not whole, not "one," except in cleaving to her. There is no room here for other women. This is the beginning and the foundation of the message of monogamy conveyed by the Bible to the polygamous society and culture of its time.

The commentators went even further, and interpreted the story of man's creation in Genesis 2 in such a fashion as to be consistent with the egalitarian version of man's male and female creation. Man was created both male and female – attached at the back, according to some *midrashim*, or at the side according to the *Zohar*. Man was alone in the sense that male and female in a single body cannot achieve sexual union. God helped them by making woman "meet" for man, i.e., in a separate body. The myth that man was created androgynous, male and female in a single body, undoubtedly conveys a clear monogamous message, entirely rejecting polygamy. The subject at hand is not creation however, but rather the monogamous message conveyed by the Bible to polygamous cultures, and that message is not weakened even by the simple meaning of the version of creation presented in Genesis 2. On the contrary, it is reinforced, and afforded independent validity, as if to say that monogamy does not necessarily stem from equality.

Abraham did in fact have a concubine, or a concubine and another wife, as noted above. The biblical narrative however does not discuss his relationships with Hagar or Keturah. On the other hand, the reader is left with a very strong impression of his relationship with Sarah. This relationship takes a broad, central and important place in the story of Abraham's life. Of the 11 verses describing Abram's journey to Egypt, nine relate to Abram and Sarai's pretending to be brother and sister, and the consequences of their ploy – one which they later repeated in the kingdom of Abimelech. Being unable to bear him children, Sarai suggests that Abram take her handmaid Hagar as a concubine: "And Sarai said unto Abram, Behold now the Lord hath restrained me from bearing: I pray thee, go in unto my maid; it may be that I may obtain children by her. And Abram hearkened to the voice of Sarai. From Sarai's point of view, Hagar was to serve as a kind of surrogate, to give birth to a son whom she would then raise. Abram is passive, expressing neither joy nor enthusiasm, but merely obeying his wife. When Hagar conceives, and begins to exhibit independent behavior, to the point that "her mistress was despised in her eyes," Sarai complains to Abram, and he responds: "Behold, thy maid is in thy hand; do to her as it pleaseth thee..." – in other words, I have no interest in her, or lasting relationship with her. What passed between us, was by your initiative, and therefore pertains only to the relationship between us. You are my only wife, even if I have known Hagar and she has conceived a child by me. Abram and Sarai's different approaches might be attributed to the fact that Abram still believed God's promise that he would grant him progeny, as it is written: "And he believed in the Lord; and he counted it to him for righteousness," whereas Sarai had given up hope of conceiving at such an advanced age. Their different attitudes are clearly reflected in their respective reactions to the message brought by the angels: "And he said, I will certainly return unto thee according to the time of life; and, lo, Sarah thy wife shall have a son...." While Abraham accepts the prediction, the Bible stresses Sarah's skepticism: "Therefore Sarah laughed within herself, saying, After I am waxed old shall I have pleasure, my lord being old also?"

The first crisis in the relationship between Abraham and Sarah again concerns Hagar: "And Sarah saw the son of Hagar the Egyptian, which she had born unto Abraham, mocking. Wherefore she said unto Abraham, Cast out this bondwoman and her son: for the son of this bondwoman shall not be heir with my son, even with Isaac.. And the thing was very grievous in Abraham's sight because of his son. And God said unto Abraham, Let it not be grievous in thy sight because of the lad, and because of thy bond-woman; in all that Sarah hath said unto thee, hearken unto her voice; for in Isaac shall thy seed be called." One cannot help but notice the marked change in Abraham's attitude. On the previous occasion, he reacted to the fate of his pregnant handmaiden with equanimity, allowing Sarah to do to with her as she saw fit. Now, "the thing was very grievous in Abraham's sight," no less. It is important to note however, that this concern is entirely directed toward his son and not to the boy's mother, and it is God who responds: "Let it not be grievous in thy sight because of the lad, and because of thy bondwoman," as if reminding Abraham that there is another person involved, also worthy of concern, and that He would in fact look after them both: "And also of the son of the bondwoman will I make a nation, because he is thy seed." The final narrative worthy of attention in the context of the relationship between Abraham and Sarah is that of Sarah's death, and Abraham's efforts to bury her – described in no less than 20 verses.

Beyond the profound sadness that envelops Abraham – "and Abraham came to mourn for Sarah, and to weep for her" – her death also marks his own demise, since he cannot live without her, and her grave will also become his. He will do one final thing following her death: he will send a slave to find a wife for his son Isaac. Once this task is completed, and Sarah's tent is once again inhabited, Abraham will join his wife in their final resting place: "And his sons... buried him... in the field... which Abraham purchased of the sons of Heth: there was Abraham buried, and

Sarah his wife." The Cave of Machpelah (from the Hebrew root KF"L, meaning twofold) is so named, according to tradition, because it is the tomb of the couples: Adam and Eve; Abraham and Sarah; Isaac and Rebekah; Jacob and Leah. This too further strengthens the message of monogamy. Abraham's entire adult life, from maturity to old age, is characterized by full partnership with, and absolute loyalty to his one and only partner: Sarah.

Nevertheless, Hagar's presence cannot be ignored. The paradigm for future generations is therefore not Abraham, and certainly not Jacob, who had two wives and two concubines, but rather Isaac. Isaac is portrayed in the Torah as the paragon of stability and virtue. He, who was bound by his father to the altar as an unblemished sacrifice, never breaks his connection with the Land. Unlike his father Abraham, Isaac never leaves the Land, even in times of famine and hardship. Nor does he break his connection with one woman, Rebekah, even during difficult and trying times, remaining in this as well, a symbol of marital fidelity. Their relationship is not merely the result of an arrangement negotiated by Eliezer on behalf of Abraham, but is founded upon love kindled at their very first meeting. At least for Rebekah it was "love at first sight." When she saw Isaac, and did not yet know who he was: "And Rebekah lifted up her eye, and when she saw Isaac, she lighted off the camel. For she had said unto the servant, What man is this that walketh in the field to meet us? And the servant had said, It is my master: therefore she took a veil, and covered herself" (Gen 24:64–65).

The Bible shares with us, a romantic and moving moment. They, Rebekah and Abraham's servant Eliezer, have traveled a long way together. The Bible skips over the story of the journey, but takes the trouble to describe the first meeting of Isaac and Rebekah – a chance meeting of the intended couple. Isaac impresses Rebekah greatly from the first moment she lays eyes on him – an encounter that moves her so deeply, that she falls off the camel. This image is touching and amusing (to the readers); Rebekah however is not amused, but probably embarrassed. Let us consider her situation for a moment. She rides a long way to meet her future husband, a man she does not know, and she does so not because she is forced to, but of her own free will ("And they said, We will call the damsel, and enquire at her mouth. And they called Rebekah, and said unto her, Wilt thou go with this man? and she said, I will go." *ibid.* 57–58). During the course of her long journey, she must have given a great deal of thought to the new life awaiting her as a married woman, and wondered considerably about her husband to be: What does he look like? What kind of person is he? What will her life be like.

At the very end of the trip, Rebekah happens to see a man, who so impresses and moves her, resulting in that embarrassing fall. What went through her mind at that moment? Did she pray that he might be the one she had been promised to? Or perhaps the opposite – that her future husband might not see her in such a state? The Bible does not tell us what she was thinking. It only tells us that Rebekah immediately wished to know who that impressive man coming toward her was, and she did so openly, asking the servant who had been charged with the task of bringing her to his master – her future husband: "What man is this that walketh in the field to meet us?" When she discovered who he was, she responds by covering herself. Is this an indication of her embarrassment, shyness, or perhaps the reaction of a woman who has fallen in love at first sight?

For Isaac as well, this is not mere "taking," but a relationship based from the outset on love. The Bible does not give us the usual terse description of so-and-so who took so-and-so for a wife, but emphasizes a process that occurred between the two, the height of which can be seen in a love that fills all of the previous voids: "And Isaac brought her into his mother Sarah's tent, and took Rebekah, and she became his wife; and he loved her: and Isaac was comforted after his mother's death" (Gen 24:67). This marriage, based from the very beginning on love, displaced every previous feeling of absence or loss, establishing a strong foundation for a perfect relationship.

As with Abraham, and even more so, Isaac's relationship with Rebekah lies at the heart of his life story. Isaac's marriage to one woman is not merely a fact, speaking for itself to whatever extent possible, but a central and highlighted message in the biblical narrative of his life. The two do not always see eye to eye, but they complement each other. In all of the events described following their marriage, the presence of both is always felt: when they are staying with Abimelech at the time of the famine; in their negative (and identical) feelings about Esau's wives; in their (different) attitudes to their sons, Esau and Jacob. It is in fact the latter, an example of disagreement between them, that makes the story of their relationship more real and believable. Love is not a state of complete compatibility and agreement, and it is not conditional upon a lack of disagreement. The Bible wishes to emphasize Isaac's loyalty to Rebekah, in that even when she was unable to bear him a child, he did not take another wife, as was the custom, but chooses rather to focus on prayer: "And Isaac entreated the Lord for his wife, because she was barren" (Gen 25:21).

Why did he need to pray? He could have done the simplest and most common thing when a first wife is found to be barren: take a second! or at least a concubine or a handmaiden. That is what all of the men around him did when they found themselves married to a barren woman. That is what his father did, and what is more, it was at his mother's instigation. Does the Torah teach us that Abraham of his own initiative prayed to God, entreating him for sons?

Isaac's unusual behavior was not, as far as we know, emulated by his son. He did not pray when his beloved wife Rachel bore him no children, being satisfied with the offspring of her sister and co-wife Leah. Moreover, he treats her rather callously: "And when

Rachel saw that she bare Jacob no children, Rachel envied her sister; and said unto Jacob, Give me children, or else I die. And Jacob's anger was kindled against Rachel: and he said, Am I in God's stead, who hath withheld from thee the fruit of the womb?" (Gen 30:1–2).

The result of this dispute between Jacob and Rachel: another wife-handmaid for Jacob – Bilhah.

Isaac was indeed unusual in his great love for Rebekah, special in his loyalty to her. He entreated God "for/before his wife" ("*lenokhah ishto*"), who was always before him, the only possible female presence in his life. Even for the sake of procreation and continuity, a matter of paramount importance, he never considered giving up this loyalty.

The patriarchs play important symbolical historical roles in the eyes of future generations, and Isaac and Rebekah well express this symbolism in its purest form, largely due to their stable, loving relationship. The paradigm presented by Isaac and Rebekah stresses to us once again that while polygamy was an expression of prevailing culture at the time, worthy love between the sexes is that which is attained in marriage between one man and one woman.

The ideal relationship between lovers, and violations of such a relationship, are an endless source of imagery in the Wisdom Books and the Prophets. The prophets employed love and the monogamous relationship to describe spiritual experiences and convey religious messages, and as an expression of the bond between God and the People of Israel. Great intensity is ascribed to first love, young love, love of the betrothed, love between bride and groom. The memory of this formidable bond helps sustain husband and wife (God and his People) through periods of crisis, and it is to this bond they strive to return when the relationship is once again on sound footing: "Thou shalt no more be termed Forsaken, neither shall thy land any more be termed Desolate; but thou shalt be called, My delight is in her, and thy land, Espoused;

for the Lord delighteth in thee, and thy land shall be espoused. For as a young man espouseth a virgin, so shall thy sons espouse thee; and as the bridegroom rejoiceth over the bride, so shall thy God rejoice over thee" (Is 62:2–4)

In these verses, the couple metaphor is twofold: God is the male – the bridegroom – and the People of Israel the bride. The Land of Israel is female and her sons return to her with the vigor of nascent love between a young man and a virgin. The main theme in both relationships described by the prophet is novelty and freshness: as a "young man" (= virgin) espouses a "virgin" – rekindling the initial passion between the People and the Land of Israel; and as a "bridegroom" rejoices in his "bride" – awakening the incipient love between God and His People.

Jeremiah, in the following famous verses, also compares God to a bridegroom returning the love of His bride Israel: "Thus saith the Lord; I remember thee, the kindness of thy youth, the love of thine espousals, when thou wentest after me in the wilderness, in a land that was not sown" (Jer 2:1–2).

"The kindness of thy youth" expresses freshness and purity. "The love of thine espousals" provides the ardor of devotion, the strength required to ignore the hardships of the desert. Memory of that first and absolute love, ensures the success of the relationship – or in its allegorical sense: redemption. It expresses not only the kindness of God, recalling his bride's devotion, but also God's loyalty to his beloved, whom love has exalted to a level at which she too can bestow kindness upon her beloved – even if he is God. During the difficult journey through the desert, in a land not sown, you could have left me, but you showed me kindness, "the kindness of thy youth," sustained by "the love of thine espousals."

This relationship is monogamous in essence, but is violated by one of the partners: the woman who betrays her divine husband and commits adultery with other lover-gods. Any assertion that God may have deserted his People are rejected outright: "But Zion said, The Lord hath forsaken me, and my Lord hath forgotten me. Can a woman forget her suckling child, that she should not have compassion on the son of her womb? yea, they may forget, yet I will not forget thee"(Is 49:14–15). Images of Israel as a treacherous woman and a harlot abound in the prophecies of Jeremiah ("… that which backsliding Israel hath done … there hath played the harlot … yet her treacherous sister Judah feared not, but went and played the harlot also" – Jer 3:6–7), Isaiah ("How is the faithful city become an harlot!"), and most prominently Hosea, in which the metaphor of harlotry and betrayal is a central theme. Nevertheless, it is Hosea who provides us with one of the most fascinating expressions of return from adultery and harlotry to a loving and faithful relationship which, like the examples above, looks forward to the relationship's glorious beginning, the period of betrothal: And it shall be at that day, saith the Lord, that thou shalt call me 'my husband' (*ishi*); and shalt call me no more 'my master' (*ba'ali*). For I will take away the names of Baalim out of her mouth, and they shall no more be remembered by their name … And I will betroth thee unto me for ever; yea, I will betroth thee unto me in righteousness, and in judgment, and in lovingkindness, and in mercies. I will even betroth thee unto me in faithfulness: and thou shalt know the Lord" (Hos 18–19; 21–22).

One cannot help but presume that the proposed change from perceiving one's partner as 'master' (*ba'al*) to perceiving him as 'husband,' is far more than a play on words and remonstration against the *Ba'alim* – the gods with which Israel had committed "adultery." It would not be too much of an anachronism to say that the language of husband-wife/man-woman (*ish-ishah*) expresses a greater state of equality between the partners, and what is more – the uniqueness of each partner to the other, than the term master-possessor, which gives sanction to the husband's possessing other women and the wife's seeking other masters. From the prophet's point of view, there can be no room for polygamous

relations, and love between the sexes is manifested in monogamous, one-woman-one-man relations: "And I will betroth thee
unto me for ever"!

The use of images and metaphors of love between the sexes
to convey spiritual and religious messages, demonstrates the
importance, centrality and deep significance ascribed to such
relationships. Love between men and women is portrayed in the
ancient sources as the most significant phenomenon in human life,
to the point that it serves as a primary source of imagery in describing transcendence from the human to the divine.

We use "the divine" in its usual sense, to express the yearning
of man or a people for God. It is also however an expression of
the bond, aspiration and yearning man feels toward wisdom and
ideas and the search for them, as reflected in the book of Proverbs
(4:5–8) and many other places. These same sources however,
constantly reiterate the message of monogamy, while voicing
criticism of male tendencies toward polygamy:

"Drink waters out of thine own cistern, and running waters
out of thine own well. Let thy fountains be dispersed abroad, and
rivers of waters in the streets ... Let thy fountain be blessed: and
rejoice with the wife of thy youth. Let her be as the loving hind and
pleasant roe; let her breast satisfy thee at all times; and be thou
ravished always with her love. And why wilt thou, my son, be
ravished with a strange woman, and embrace the bosom of a
stranger?" (Prov 5:15–20).

Wisdom is compared to water, and its attainment requires
perseverance and fidelity. It is difficult at first, evoking images of
"when thou wentest after me in the wilderness, in a land that was
not sown" and "Who led thee through the great and terrible
wilderness, wherein were fiery serpents, and scorpions, and
drought, where there was no water" (Deut 8:15). It must be collected in a cistern or drawn from a well, but if you are loyal to your
own cistern or well, you will profit therefrom. You yourself be-

come a fountain of knowledge, whence it is dispersed abroad to all who wish to drink of it. While the image of the unfaithful wife abounds in the Prophets, Proverbs ascribes such perfidy to the man, whom it exhorts ("rejoice with the wife of thy youth") to be faithful to his one and only love, and whom it admonishes for embracing a stranger. The relationship portrayed here rejects any possibility of polygamy, and strengthens the biblical message of monogamy.

These verses from Proverbs, like others in the Bible, some of which have been cited here, attach great importance and centrality to monogamous relationships. This centrality is not reflected however in the precepts of the Torah, which include neither a negative injunction against polygamy nor a positive commandment to practice monogamy. The Torah merely presents a rather broad system of sexual prohibition (Lev 18; 20) that slightly narrowed the possibilities, limiting the number of women available for marriage to those for whom they are forbidden. This would have been significant in a society with a tribal-family structure, since marriage within the extended family would have been easier than marriage between members of different extended families or tribes, which would have involved more complex monetary arrangements and difficulties concerning inheritance. Gradually and indirectly, the system of sexual prohibitions had a certain influence on the reduction of polygamy.

The Torah also provided the option of divorce for cases in which marital harmony has come to an end (Deut 24:1). Allowing divorce is a fundamental statement in favor of monogamy, with far-reaching ramifications regarding the importance of relations between the sexes. In a polygamous culture, a man is not expected to live in harmony with all or even one of his wives. The polygamous ethic is not based on love and mutuality, and at most addresses the man's ability to provide for and protect his wives against the aggression of others. The Torah in fact does not forbid polygamy, but in allowing divorce, it introduced the issue of marital harmony into the heart of polygamous culture. It is done by negation, but one cannot ignore the force of this realistic position and its potential influence on attitudes toward relations between men and women within the framework of marriage. Allowing divorce is in effect a statement in support of monogamy: If the relationship doesn't work out, taking another wife in addition to the first one is not a recommended course of action. As difficult as such a course of action may be in a patriarchal society, it is better to divorce the first wife and only then to marry another, rather than to have more than one wife at a time.

Polygamy is also portrayed as a recipe for strife and hatred:

"If a man have two wives, one beloved, and another hated, and they have born him children, both the beloved and the hated; and if the firstborn son be hers that was hated ... he may not make the son of the beloved firstborn before the son of the hated, which is indeed the firstborn. But he shall acknowledge the son of the hated for the firstborn ..." (Deut 21:15–17).

According to the Torah, the practically inevitable consequence of a man's having two wives is that one will be beloved and the other hated. The difficult relationships within such a family are a given, even if they come to a head only later when there are disputes between the sons of the two wives over their father's inheritance. The Torah does not forbid marriage to more than one woman, but it certainly sees the problems posed by such relationships.

The passage in the book of Deuteronomy that deals with the appointment of a king is one of the most fascinating and controversial in the Torah. The commentators argue whether the appointment of a king is mandatory or merely permitted. All agree however the sovereign described in Deuteronomy – unlike his counterparts in other nations – is bound by certain restrictions: "When thou art come unto the land which the Lord thy God giveth thee, and shalt possess it, and shalt dwell therein, and shalt say, I will set a king over me, like as all the nations that are about me; Thou shalt in any wise set him king over thee, whom the Lord thy God shall choose: one from among thy brethren shalt thou set king over thee: thou mayest not set a stranger over thee, which is not thy brother. But he shall not multiply horses to himself, nor cause the people to return to Egypt, to the end that he should multiply horses: forasmuch as the Lord hath said unto you, Ye shall henceforth return no more that way. Neither shall he multiply wives to himself, that his heart turn not away: neither shall he greatly multiply to himself silver and gold" (Deut 17:14–17).

One of the above prohibitions has bearing on the subject we are investigating: Kings are charged not to have many wives. This prohibition reflects an attempt to change the polygamous behavior of the king, who serves as a role-model for society as a whole. This can be seen as an attempt to effect socio-cultural change, from a polygamy to a monogamy – or at least to a less polygamous society. The biblical injunction does not seek to prevent a king from taking more than one wife, but imposes a certain limitation upon one who had never been limited before. On the contrary, the very fact that he was king had enabled him, more than any other man, to have as many wives and concubines as he saw fit. Kings would have many wives in their palaces as an expression of control, power, political alliances, and a source of images and legends about them. The prohibition against a king of Israel's taking many wives also raised the question: What is "many"? The Rabbis discussed this issue without stressing the innovation in limiting a king's right to take as many wives as he wished. Regarding the question of whether this prohibition stems from the Torah's desire to restrict polygamy to some extent, or from the fear that his wives would cause his "heart to turn away" from God, there is some disagreement in the Mishnah: " 'Neither shall he multiply wives to himself' – but only eighteen. Rabbi Judah said: He may multiply [wives], as long as they do not turn his heart away. Rabbi Simon said: Even if one will turn his heart away, he may not marry her. Why then is it written (Deut 17) 'Neither shall he multiply wives to himself'? Even [if they are] as Abigail" (*Sanhedrin* 2, 4).

The sages of the Mishnah were fully aware of the biblical sources that chastise Solomon in this matter (I Kings 11:1–3), but fail to criticize other kings, who may not have had harems like that of Solomon, but who certainly had numerous wives. The numerical limit imposed by the Mishnah was inspired by King David, who had 6 wives and 12 concubines. It is unclear whether the prophet simply states the fact that David had 18 wives, or establishes that number as being in keeping with the biblical injunction imposed upon him. David serves as a source for the laws pertaining to kings, including the halakhic quantification of the prohibition against a king's "multiplying" wives. The Bathsheba affair does not mar the image of David as a righteous king and founder of Israel's dynasty of kings. Indeed the Rabbis strove to absolve David of wrongdoing, despite biblical indications to the contrary: "Rabbi Samuel bar Nahmani said in the name of Rabbi Yonatan: 'He who says David sinned is mistaken' " (*Shabbat* 56a). There is therefore no reason not to learn this *halakhah* from King David. Contrary to the general opinion cited in the *mishnah*, whereby a king may marry a maximum of 18 women, Rabbi Judah believed that a king might marry as many women as he wished – even more than 18 – on condition that they do not turn his heart away from God's commandments. Rabbi Judah's opinion is not accepted, and established *halakhah* in this matter is that a king may not take more than 18 wives. Other opinions in the Talmud, suggesting figures of 24 and even 48, are rejected. "Neither shall he multiply wives to himself" is thus not a sweeping ban. It does, however, express a basic moral position. A king of Israel is required to limit the number of wives he takes, in terms of the cultural norm, and in respecting this injunction, he serves as a paragon for the entire people.

Another figure worthy of emulation is that of the high priest. Although the Torah does not explicitly forbid the high priest to have many wives, it states that he may not marry any woman who is not a virgin, thus restricting his choice of women and hence his ability to "multiply wives": "And he that is the high priest among his brethren, upon whose head the anointing oil was poured, and that is consecrated to put on the garments … And he shall take a wife in her virginity. A widow, or a divorced woman, or profane, or an harlot, these shall he not take: but he shall take a virgin of his own people to wife. Neither shall he profane his seed among his people, for I the Lord do sanctify him" (Lev 21:10; 13–15).

As noted above, there is no biblical injunction against a high priest marrying many women – as long as they are all virgins. The Talmud however, infers such a prohibition from the Torah: " 'An atonement for himself, and for his house' (Lev 16:6) – not for two houses" (JT *Yoma* 1, 1 – 38d; *Yoma* 13a, 71a), and: " 'but he shall take a virgin of his own people to wife' (Lev 21:14) – one and not two" (*Yevamot* 59a).

We have seen that the kings failed to observe the minimal restrictions imposed upon them by the Torah. Were the high priests strictly monogamous, in keeping with the absolute prohibition against high-priestly polygamy? We have no evidence of any violation of the monogamous norm among any of the high priests. A passage worthy of closer scrutiny is: "Joash was seven years old when he began his reign, and he reigned forty years in Jerusalem. His mother's name also was Zibiah of Beersheba. And Joash did that which was right in the sight of the Lord all the days of Jehoiada the priest. And Jehoiada took for him two wives; and he begat sons and daughters. And it came to pass after this, that Joash was minded to repair the house of the Lord" (II Chron 24:1–5). This chapter tells the history of King Joash, who ruled 40 years in Jerusalem, and of the High Priest Jehoiada. It reviews the reign of King Jehoram's wife, Athaliah, who killed all of the descendants of the royal house of Judah – all of the males who might lay claim to the throne. Jehoiada the Priest conspired against Athaliah, anointed Joash – the child hidden by Jehoshabeath – thereby rising to prominence. Jehoiada's influence was great, and there is no doubt that he was the strong man in the kingdom and the only high priest reported to have been buried in the sepulchers of the kings. Among the verses pertaining to the history of Joash, we find the following: "And Jehoiada took for him two wives; and he begat sons and daughters." Some have taken the verse, detached from its context, simply to mean that the high priest was a bigamist, in contravention of the Talmudic law that forbids (by inferred biblical injunction) a high priest to marry more than one woman. As noted however, the subject of this passage is not Jehoiada, and the meaning of the above verse is that Jehoiada the priest took for Joash two wives simultaneously or in close succession, in order to enable him to beget sons and re-establish the House of David, of which he was the sole survivor, following Athaliah's massacre. Joscphus writes: "… and when he (Joash) was of age, he married two wives, who were given to him by the high priest, by whom were born to him both sons and daughters" (*Antiq.* 9, 7).

Discussion of the verse's possible, anomial meaning, confirms the importance ascribed to the high priest's obligation to practice monogamy. The injunction against the highest religious authority's marrying more than one woman, and the requirement that the king limit the number of wives he takes to the greatest extent possible, that he might serve as a role-model for the nation and its leaders – together constitute an expression of the canonical Jewish position on polygamy.

We must stress once again that polygamy was the norm at the time, and that any opposition to the norm represents a new and revolutionary approach, or in the words of Goody: "It is not polygamy that needs to be explained, but its absence; the former is common, the latter, i.e., monogamy, rare" (J. Goody, 1973, p. 176).

Monogamy thus joins all of the other revolutions the Torah sought to foment: the Sabbath, social justice, and above (and in conjunction with) all – monotheism. None of these goals can be attained all at once. They are rather, ongoing processes, offering fresh revolutionary challenges on a daily basis, in every generation, for society as a whole and for each individual member.

The rejection of polytheism parallels the departure from polygamy, and the idea of the unity of God is applied to the unification of man and woman in a single entity. While the biblical message of monotheism is accompanied by a broad system of negative and positive precepts, as well as various decrees, amendments and legal minutiae pertaining to idolatry, the message of monogamy is conveyed as an idea, a moral position, but lacking practical expression in the form of laws and precepts – beyond that which we have described above. The Torah's approach in this matter would appear to be to avoid unrealistic legislation. That is how the Torah's sanction of "And seest among the captives a beautiful woman, and hast a desire unto her ..." (Deut 21:11) is viewed, and that is perhaps how one should view the fact that the ideology of monogamy receives no clear and obvious legal expression in the Bible or the Talmud. Despite an aversion to polygamy, and recognition of the fact that man and woman can only find true fulfillment within a monogamous relationship – no attempt was made to legislate against the cultural norm, in an attempt to create a new and different constitutional standard, knowing full well that it could never withstand the test of reality in a society steeped in polygamous culture.

The absence of legislative support notwithstanding, we must not underestimate the force of the Bible's monogamous message, and the inescapable comparison with its monotheistic message. The concepts of unity and unification are essentially the same, strengthening, supporting and largely dependent upon one another. Belief in a single God, i.e., juxtaposing the individual with her/his

God within the context of the belief in unity, parallels the juxtaposition of one woman and one man; and their complete physical union within the harmony of mind and emotion parallels the idea of the unity of God.

This is, in itself, a very powerful comparison. Some however, have gone beyond merely drawing a parallel between monogamy and monotheism, asserting that the two concepts are in fact one and the same. Adherents of the latter approach maintain that monogamy in fact derives from the principle of divine unity. Kabbalistic sources do not merely cite divine unity, but – in keeping with their characteristic use of language from the realm of imagination, emotion and spirit – illustrate this unity with sexual imagery.

Love, desire and divine union in the world of the *Sefirot*, are the source of all existence, the blueprint of creation, a path for man and a connection between all worlds. The concept of the ten *Sefirot* of divinity is central to all Kabbalistic thought. The *Sefirot* appear in the *Zohar* in the form of a variety of images and attributes of the divine. One of the most well-known of these attributes and images is that of the Supreme Man (*Adam Elyon*) – an anthropomorphic image used to describe the world of the divine, to discuss it, or to make various assertions concerning it. This figure is the source of all abundance in the cosmos, an abundance that flows from the *Sefirah* of *Keter* (Crown), or from the *Sefirot* of *Hokhmah* (Wisdom), *Binah* (Intelligence), *Hesed* (Love/Mercy), *Gevurah* (Power), *Tiferet* (Beauty), *Netzah* (Eternity), *Hod* (Majesty), and *Yesod* (Foundation). The figure of the Supreme Man, which comprises all of the above *Sefirot*, is male, and its female partner is the *Sefirah* of *Malkhut* (Kingdom). The *Zohar* calls the divine male and female: God and the *Shekhinah*, or the King and Queen.

The use of sexual symbolism to represent connection and union, recurs in various forms, not only between the *Sefirot* that describe the divine world and are in turn described as the Supreme

Man – male – and *Malkhut* or the *Shekhinah*, connected with or facing the world of creation, but also within the world of the divine, at its most secret and highest levels. The two highest *Sefirot*, *Hokhmah* and *Binah*, are the father and mother of the lower *Sefirot*, created by their sexual union, and continuing to be nurtured by them (*Zohar* 1, 246b). The relationship between them is described in terms of male and female from which the world of *Atzilut* (Emanation) derives, creating harmony throughout the divine – which is based upon male and female images and the relations between them. The lower *Sefirot* existed within their father and mother, *Hokhmah* and *Binah*, and were created through their sexual union. At first, they were inside *Binah*, like a fetus in its mother's womb, then they emanated from *Binah*, which gave birth to them. Kabbalah compares the idea of emanation to the mystery of birth. Following the birth, the father and mother, the supreme couple – i.e., *Hokhmah* and *Binah* – continue to serve as a source for the lower *Sefirot*, and an example for their "behavior." The enduring, unceasing and infinite love of *Hokhmah* and *Binah* serves as an example and an inspiration. Their everlasting relationship is a paragon of love at its highest, toward which all aspire. The love of *Hokhmah* and *Binah* arouses the love of the lower *Sefirot* for one another, and creates a harmonious relationship among them as well. It is from this relationship between the lower spheres, often described as the relationship between God and the *Shekhinah* – that souls are born (*Zohar* 1, 209a; 2, 223b).

All souls are created as the product of the passion and sexual union of God and the *Shekhinah*, and comprise both the male attributes of *Tiferet*, and the female attributes of *Malkhut*:

"Come and see: All of the souls of the world, which are the fruit of God's labor, are one in the secret of one. And when they descend to the world they all separate in the form of male and female, and are male and female joined as one. And come and see: The female passion toward the male creates a spirit, and the male passion toward the female creates a spirit, and the pleasure of the male passion toward the female and his joining with her brings forth a spirit ... And when the souls go forth, they go forth male and female as one, and when they descend, they separate one to the one side and the other to the other side, and God unites them later, and [the task of] uniting them is given to no other but to God alone, who knows how to unite and join them suitably."

All souls, which are the fruit of God's labor – i.e., products of the divine sexual union, as they reside in the world of divinity, in the *Shekhinah* – are "one in the secret of one." The secret is that of unity comprising both male and female indistinguishable from one another, and the assertion that the soul is "one" signifies a unity of male and female. The female essence within the soul is created by female passion toward the male, "creating a spirit" – bestowing the female spiritual essence. The male essence within the soul is created by the male passion toward the female – bestowing the male spiritual essence. All of this occurs "in the secret of one": the secret of divine unity, which is also a unity comprising both male and female. When the soul descends to the world of creation however, the world of plurality and separation, it separates "in the form of male and female," and God unites them later.

Kabbalah is full of messages about love relationships: Not only does love exist in the world of the *Sefirot*, sustaining the divine and thus serving as a paragon for man to seek and adhere to the harmony of union between the sexes, but if the relationship between a man and a woman is successful, it is because they were created within the *Shekhinah* as a single soul, and when that soul descended to earth, it was divided in two, until reunified in their relationship. The idea of bisexuality of souls at the time of their creation in the *Shekhinah* thus has deep and far-reaching significance for the relationship between a man and a woman – who cannot attain completeness except in their union.

Kabbalah's approach to love relationships in terms of the nature of souls is uncompromising and stems from a hermetic spiritual paradigm. According to this paradigm, bachelorhood is completely untenable, even in the most exceptional circumstances. The deficiency of bachelorhood is absolute, and only love within the context of a male-female relationship – two half-souls uniting in their love – can bring man to fulfill his purpose in the world of creation and return the soul to its divine source.

Kabbalistic interpretation, in all its discussions pertaining to relations between the sexes, refers exclusively to monogamous marriage: one man and one woman, with no mention whatsoever of polygamy. The principle whereby every soul is created both male and female, separated upon descent into the world, and re-united later, makes simultaneous marriage to more than one woman completely unthinkable.

3. *Onah* – Sex not for the Sake of Procreation

There are two separate precepts that require married couples to have sex: "be fruitful and multiply" (procreation), and "*onah*" ("conjugal rights"). The former requires that a man contribute to "populating the world," the continuity of his seed, that is having children, and in this matter *Halakhah* has determined that one who has begotten a son and a daughter has fulfilled his obligation. Of course, this precept requires that one have sex with his wife during the fertile part of her cycle, at least until he has children. Sex for the sake of procreation however, is merely a means to an end.

The Torah established another precept however, unrelated to the continuity of the seed and populating the world, but to sex itself, and the marriage relationship. The *onah* obligation (Ex 21:10) requires that the husband regularly have sex with his wife – not as a means to have children, but as an end in itself, for the sake of pleasure (*Nedarim* 15b).

The frequency of this obligation is determined by the husband's physical strength, and the extent to which his work (providing for the family) allows him to be at home. One whose work enables him to spend more time with his wife is also required to have sex more frequently. As noted, this obligation has absolutely no connection to procreation, and thus applies to one who has already fulfilled the requirements of "be fruitful and multiply" and cannot have more children, on days when the woman is not fertile, and even during pregnancy. A woman has the right to demand that her husband not change his occupation to one in which he will be away from home for extended periods, or that he not go away at a certain time – since her conjugal rights would thus be affected.

The significance of *onah,* as the husband's duty to satisfy his wife, is also reflected in the specific requirement that a husband have sex with his wife before departing on a journey:

"Rabbi Joshua ben Levi said: A man must have marital relations with his wife when he departs on a journey ... This teaches us that a woman desires her husband when he departs on a journey" (*Yevamot* 62b).

The husband's duty is presented here as a direct consequence of his wife's desire. This is an important statement regarding the nature of relations between man and wife: The woman is not bound to serve her husband and satisfy his needs. It is rather the husband who must serve her and satisfy her needs.

The background behind this *halakhah* is a discussion elsewhere in the Talmud regarding women's desires and the manner in which they are expressed: " 'And thy desire shall be to thy husband' (Gen 3:16) – This teaches us that a woman desires her husband when he departs on a journey. 'And he shall rule over thee' – This teaches us that a woman demands in her heart, and a man gives voice to his demands. This is a positive quality in women, for they demonstrate affection toward their husbands" (*Eruvin* 100b).

The expression "and he shall rule over thee" is interpreted in an unusual fashion here. The sages of the Talmud charge the man with the responsibility of responding to his wife's desires, taking her nature into consideration. Unlike men, who are more wont to give full verbal expression to their desires ("a man gives voice to his demands"), a woman usually "demands in her heart," rather than explicitly voicing her desires. This is "a positive quality in women," attesting to their greater modesty. A woman's desires however, are no less ardent, and the man is therefore charged with the responsibility of responding to them. Women have their own ways of expressing desire: "they demonstrate affection toward their husbands," and expect them to understand what they mean. Women's sexual communication differs from that of men: the ways in which a woman strives to arouse her husband are delicate, and not explicit or direct like those of men. The Rabbis did not however, wish to silence women and keep them from expressing their desires. On the contrary, they encouraged women to give clear expression to their needs and desires: "Rabbi Samuel bar Nahmani said in the name of Rabbi Johanan: A woman who demands marital relations of her husband will have sons the like of which did not exist even in the generation of Moses. Of Moses' generation it is written 'Take you wise men, and understanding, and known among your tribes' (Deut 1:13), and it is written 'So I took the chief of your tribes, wise men and known' (*ibid.* 15), and 'understanding men' could not be found. Of Leah however, it is written 'and Leah went out to meet him, and said, Thou must come in unto me; for surely I have hired thee' (Gen 30:16), and it is written 'And of the children of Issachar, which were men that had understanding of the times, to know what Israel ought to do' (I Chron 12:33)" (*Eruvin ibid.*).

Leah, wife of Jacob, demanded that her husband have sex with her, after she had hired him from her sister and co-wife Rachel, for the night, with her son's mandrakes. Leah is presented here as a role-model for women, who are called upon to act as she did, for she did not restrain her desire, but demanded that her husband satisfy her. Not only did she insist upon exercising her basic right, by virtue of her husband's *onah* obligation, but the Rabbis even reinforce such behavior, claiming that such intercourse, initiated by the woman, will produce splendid children "the like of which did not exist even in the generation of Moses"! Moses sought men possessing three important leadership qualities – wise, understanding and known – but could find only men with two of these qualities. No understanding men could be found. Intercourse between Leah and Jacob on that night, initiated by Leah, produced Issachar, whose descendants are described in the Bible as "men that had understanding of the times" – indeed "the like of which did not exist even in the generation of Moses."

It is interesting to note that in the traditional sources, "understanding" is considered a female quality. It is written in the Talmud: "God granted women greater understanding than men" (*Sotah* 38b). It is apparently for this reason that the Rabbis believed that when sex is initiated by the woman, there is a greater chance that sons born of such a union will inherit their mother's understanding.

According to talmudic law, the obligation of *onah*, sex for the sake of pleasure, requires "proximity" of the flesh – direct physical contact between the man and the woman: "Rabbi Joseph taught: '*She'erah*' (Ex 21:10) means proximity of the flesh, that he may not do as the Persians, who have marital relations in their garments. Rabbi Huna offers further support, for Rabbi Huna said: He who says I will not have marital relations unless I am clothed and she is clothed, must divorce his wife and give her the benefits stipulated in her marriage contract" (*Ketubot* 48a).

Rabbi Joseph, an *amora* (later talmudic sage), reported an earlier (tannaitic) tradition, whereby in addition to a man's obligation to have sex with his wife, i.e., *onah*, the Torah also stipulated the manner in which he must do so. The Torah requires "proximity of the flesh" – inferred from the word "*she'erah*" (Ex 21:10). Based on this teaching, Rabbi Huna ruled that a man who refuses to have marital relations when both partners are naked, but insists rather that they be clothed, should be compelled to divorce his wife and pay her the amount promised to her in the marriage contract. Even the assumption that he does so for "reasons of modesty" does not stand in his favor, and he is considered to have violated his obligation toward his wife partner. This *halakhah* reinforces the understanding that *onah* was established as a distinct obligation for the sake of sexual pleasure, since the obligation to procreate does not require the partners to be naked.

Further support for the Rabbis' position whereby *onah* is a fundamental part of love and harmony between marriage partners, can be deduced from the laws concerning a "rebellious wife" – a woman who refuses to have sex with her husband. If the reason she has refused is because she despises him, he is compelled to divorce her, "for she is not as a captive, to lie with one whom she despises." Behind this law is the principle of a woman's right to a satisfying sex life, including the right to refuse to have sex with a man she does not love. The "rebellious wife," whose behavior is by definition negative, appears here to be a woman who stands up for her rights, and *Halakhah* recognizes that, requiring that she be released from a marriage to a man she does not want. The Rabbis blame the husband for her refusal, and utterly reject the possibility of sexual relations without her consent, as we see in the following passage, as well: "Rami bar Hama said in the name of Rabbi Assi: A man may not coerce his wife to have marital relations, as it is written 'and he that hasteneth with his feet sinneth' (Prov 19:20). And Rabbi Joshua ben Levi said: He who coerces his wife to have marital relations will have indecent sons … We have also learned: 'Also that the soul be without knowledge, it is not good' (*ibid.*) – That is one who coerces his wife to have marital relations. 'And he that hasteneth with his feet sinneth' – That is one who has intercourse twice. But how could that be? For Rava said: He who wishes to have male children should have intercourse twice? The latter case is with consent, and the former without consent" (*Eruvin ibid.*).

The Talmud rules that a husband may not coerce his wife to have marital relations (referred to in the Talmud as "fulfilling the commandment"). That is not the way in which to fulfill one's obligation to procreate. In order to reinforce the prohibition, the Talmud cites the words of Rabbi Joshua ben Levi, who asserts that non-consensual relations will produce indecent sons who will not be a source of pride to their father. It is interesting to compare this threat to sinners, with the Talmud's promise to a woman who demands sex (also referred to as "fulfilling the commandment") of her husband, that she will have sons "the like of which did not exist even in Moses' generation" (see above).

The Talmud also makes a clear distinction between one who has intercourse a second time without his wife's consent and is considered a sinner, and one who does so with his wife's consent – undoubtedly with the common hope of having male offspring. In various talmudic and midrashic sources, the sex of a child is said to depend upon which parent achieves sexual satisfaction first: "Rabbi Isaac said in the name of Rabbi Ami: If the woman climaxes first, she will give birth to a son. If the man climaxes first, she will give birth to a daughter" (*Nidah* 25b, 31a). Since the birth of a son is considered preferable, men are thus encouraged to concern themselves with their wives' sexual satisfaction. The commentators explain that when the second act is consensual, the chances that the woman will climax first are greater, since her desire will have been aroused by the first act. Nevertheless, as we learn from the case of Jacob and Leah, when both partners climax together, there is a greater chance of having twins: a boy and a girl.

Onah – sex for the sake of pleasure – is founded upon shared intention, mutual consent. This obligation is referred to in the Talmud as "the joy of *onah*" (*Pesahim* 72b), since mutual consent and shared pleasure will bring the partners sublime joy.

The stabilizing element in love, as it appears in a number of place in the *Zohar*, is joy. A man must ensure that there is a joyous atmosphere in his relationship with his wife in general, avoiding sadness and strife, but particularly during their sexual union. The *Zohar* sharply criticizes one who has sex in an atmosphere of sadness and strife, to the extent that it compares such conduct to illicit sexual relations (*Tikkunei Zohar*, introd., 4a). This is a condemnation of one who has sex reluctantly, for fear of committing a supposedly "unspiritual" act. Sex is first and foremost a religious duty, and as such is treated as a joyous occasion. The *Zohar* completely rejects the notion that expressions of human physicality should be treated as "base" needs. The joy expresses release and religious exaltation, raising the physical act to a high plane, by means of the strongest human emotions, and not merely by intellectual reasoning. True union between man and woman cannot be attained without joy: "A man must therefore gladden his wife at that time, invite her, in a single desire with him, and they must share the same intention; and when the two are together then all is one in soul and in body. In soul, to cleave one to the other in a single desire. And in body, as we have learned, a man who is not married is like half a body, and when male and female are joined, they become one body. They are thus one soul and one body, and are called one person. Then God descends upon the one and imbues that one with a holy spirit, and they are called God's children, as it is written. And thus 'Ye shall be holy: for I the Lord your God am holy' " (*Zohar* 3, 81b).

Sex in itself can arouse joy naturally, but here a man is told not to take this for granted, but to make a deliberate effort to bring joy to his wife. Joy is the basis – the substructure upon which complete harmony in sexual union is built. It will help a man to bring his wife to desire it as he does, and to co-ordinate their intentions. Joy contributes to comprehensive and sweeping unity. It fosters unity of will and intention, and renders the moment of sexual union one of unity of body and soul, complete and utter harmony. In this, joy is the actualizing force of love between the partners.

Refusal by one of the partners to have sex is cause for divorce, since regular sex for the sake of pleasure establishes harmony in married life. Lack of physical attraction is sufficient cause for divorce.

Sexual desire is presented in many traditional sources as a sublime quality, associated with the highest human expression of "knowing" and "remembering": " 'And Adam knew his wife again,' desire was added to his desire. Previously he had no desire unless he saw her" (*Midrash Rabbah* Gen 23, 5). Adam's attaining the level of knowledge is reflected in the fact that his desire for his partner had risen to a higher plane. Now he "knew her" – desire became a matter of consciousness, and he desired her even in her absence, even when he could not see her.

The language of the *midrash* is reminiscent of the reflections of the Greek philosophers on the concept of "*orexis*" – desire associated with memory and knowledge. Desire is so important that there is a special angel appointed over it (*Midrash Rabbah* Gen 53, 6); and above all, it brings harmony and peace between the partners: "That is desire, which establishes peace between man and his wife" (*Midrash Rabbah* Lev 18, 1).

Desire is essential to a complete relationship between man and wife. In cases of disagreements, arguments and even fights, matters are not always resolved verbally, and the physical bond plays a crucial role in establishing peace between them, making for a healthy and complete relationship. Relationships will always have ups and downs, and sex plays a vital role in improving relations, particularly during the downs. Investing in the physical relationship, having sex for the sake of pleasure, is a very worthy matter, according to *Halakhah*, and it is one of the ways in which to ensure success in married life.

This approach, whereby desire is seen as a positive human quality, is reflected in many other traditional sources, which assert that the creator did not instill any negative impulses in man. Man possesses the freedom to choose to act in a positive or negative manner, and he may use natural impulses such as desire or jealousy, for good – deepening the bond with his wife; or for bad – engaging in illicit sex, and causing suffering to his wife.

The obligation of *Onah* – whereby a man is required to have sex with his wife for the sake of pleasure, and is charged with the responsibility of ensuring her pleasure – is a central expression of feminist innovation and revolution in the canonical sources. The status of women in talmudic times or even a thousand years later did not require the development of a halakhic, practical and behavioral approach of this kind. The obligation of *onah* was not a natural outgrowth of prevailing culture, but rather a determination aimed at changing social reality and hierarchy between the sexes. It stems from a deep moral conviction that women were not meant merely to serve men. This conviction ran contrary to the norm, which saw women as bound to serve their husbands, and marital relations were referred to in Hebrew as "*tashmish hamitah*" – "bed-service" (an expression that could in fact be understood in two ways: she serves him, but he also serves her).

The moral principle that women were not meant merely to serve their husbands has independent merit of course, but in the context of relationships it is also rooted in understanding of the concept of love. Love has the power to sweep aside disparity and differences of class, to ignore hierarchy, and to create a state of equality for those who are touched by it. The canonical sources we have seen here, view the marriage relationship as one founded upon love. Love would appear to rise above the common rules, having the power to change cultural reality at a given time and place. Love, in this sense, rises above law and accepted norm, raising up those who would otherwise have been considered inferior. It has the ability, as in the case of *onah*, to change the norm and create a new law. The obligation of *onah*, mandating sex for the sake of pleasure and stressing the woman's pleasure, is a revolutionary law, which not only does not stem from the normative culture, but actually collides with it. Consequently, traditional sources tend to ignore it, or to incorporate it into the obligation to procreate. In this sense, there is a discrepancy between the general creative and literary discourse on the subject of *onah*, and its actual fulfillment by loving couples, over millennia. Normative culture did not allow *onah* to take an independent place in literature, but apart from the fact that it is plainly a matter of some delicacy, its rightful place is indeed within the intimacy of marriage, and it has no place in the center-stage of public discourse.

It is no coincidence that the right to sexual pleasure has been a fundamental part of feminist ideology in the modern era, and there are those who see it as one of the most important expressions of the feminist revolution. This fact can help give us an appropriate sense of proportion when we learn about the application of a similar principle that developed in talmudic law and subsequent halakhic literature, hundreds and thousands of years before the feminist revolution.

4. The Love Relationship as an Expression of Perfection

The *Midrash* constantly reiterates the belief that perfect man, the "crowning glory of creation," comprises both genders – male and female. The height of this perfection lies not only in the marriage relationship, but in sexual intercourse between them, a physical manifestation perceived as spiritual perfection on a human plane and in the upper worlds. Great significance is ascribed to "populating the world" – continuity of the species, expressed in the commandment to "be fruitful and multiply" – but there is nothing new in that. What is unique about the Rabbis' approach is the importance it ascribes to the relationship itself, unrelated to procreation: "Although a man may have a number of sons, he must not be without a wife" (*Yevamot* 61b). Being "without a wife" would make him incomplete. This wholeness is not related to procreation, but rather to the harmony one can attain only as a couple. The unique element in the Rabbis' approach is not their objection to distinguishing between spiritual and physical love, or their rejection of the concepts of "original sin" and celibacy. These positions stem from a unique belief that sees perfection in the relationship between man and woman, and lays the foundation for the ideal of love.

In this discussion of harmony and reciprocity, it is important to remind ourselves once again, that all of the texts, without exception, were written from a male perspective. "*Adam*" (man) in rabbinical terms is a male, and it is he who "must not be without a wife." It is the man whose being single will deny him everything good in this world. The man is an incomplete, divided "*adam*," if he lives without a woman. Although we can assume that women also benefit and gain wholeness through marriage, the traditional sources emphasize the fact that it is she who complements him. It is therefore surprising that this does not preclude the development of positions advocating reciprocal harmony in love between man and woman. This can be explained in light of the Rabbis' approach to the biblical messages in this matter. It is possible, and even desirable to infuse the old sources with new and valid meanings, and to highlight rabbinical statements upon which we can base relationships between the sexes in our own cultural and social environment. In order to avoid currently popular anachronistic approaches to the traditional sources, discovering feminism and supposedly egalitarian views in rabbinical literature, I feel it is important to stress the true content of the sources and their precise cultural context. It is conceivable that refusing to ignore the original meaning of the texts, may make the messages they convey even more meaningful and revolutionary. In this sense we can see the Rabbis as doing more than just conveying their contemporary culture. They are the bearers of change to those who follow their teachings and to Jewish society as a whole.

The *Midrash* lists every possible deficiency of a man who lives alone: "Rabbi Jacob taught: He who has no wife dwells without good, without help, without joy, without blessing, without atonement. Without good – 'It is not good that the man should be alone' (Gen 1:18). Without help – 'I will make him an help meet for him' (*ibid.*). Without joy – 'And thou shalt rejoice, thou, and thine household' (Deut 14:26). Without blessing – 'That he may cause the blessing to rest in thine house' (Ezek 44:30). Without atonement – 'And shall make an atonement for himself, and for his house' (Lev 16:11). Rabbi Simon said in the name of Rabbi Joshua ben Levi: Without peace as well, as it is written: 'Peace be both to thee, and peace be to thine house' (I Sam 25:6). Rabbi Joshua of Siknin said in the name of Rabbi Levi: Without life as well, as it is written: 'Live joyfully with the wife whom thou lovest' (Ecc 9:9)" (*Midrash Rabbah*, Gen 17, 2).

The list presented by the *midrash* includes central elements that give life meaning: good, help (= support), joy, atonement, blessing, peace, and of course life itself.

All of these things are enjoyed by married men and are lacking in the lives of those who "have no wife." Some of these things can be direct consequences of a harmonious relationship, for example help, that is mutual support or companionship, which is the opposite of "man being alone"; and joy, which certainly results from a love relationship, and in turn, enriches the relationship itself. Other components, according to the Rabbis, would seem to depend upon divine blessing: good, atonement, blessing and peace – and these are not bestowed upon one who lives alone. One who is not married is deemed unworthy of these blessings! This approach is the complete opposite of the Christian concept of "original sin," which perceives something inherently negative in married life, possibly requiring constant atonement; it is certainly inconceivable that a Christian would be denied atonement because of his celibacy. According to the Rabbis, marriage is a fundamental obligation and the purpose of life, and God does not give atonement for other sins to one who does not fulfill this commandment, but rather chooses to live alone.

Rabbi Simon in the name of Rabbi Joshua ben Levi, adds a further component to the bachelor's list of deficiencies: "Without peace as well." The concept of peace can be seen as the sum total of all of the previous elements without which man is incomplete. Rabbi Joshua ben Levi however, well-known for his statements concerning the importance and centrality of peace in general, makes no distinction between human perfection and peace. He sees personal peace – that which exists within the family unit – as the basis for peace between people and throughout the world. The bachelor, who lacks peace, is vulnerable to his passions, and may therefore channel his energies into fighting and war. Married life is thus the basis for peace throughout society.

Based on all of the above, the conclusion of Rabbi Joshua of Siknin that the life of a man without a woman is not life, is unavoidable. Reality beyond the framework of a monogamous relationship is pointless, and man is not whole except as a couple – man and woman – who together create a single perfection: "Rabbi Hiyya bar Gamda said: Nor is he a complete man, as it is written: "And he blessed them, and called their name *Adam*" – the two together are called *Adam*" (*Midrash Rabbah, ibid.*).

Rabbi Hiyya bar Gamda bases his words on the verse in Genesis that notes that the name "*Adam*" is the shared name of man and woman, and that only their union in marriage can ensure perfection. Despite the semantic convention of calling only man "*adam*," Rabbi Hiyya reminds us that only "the two together" – when they are together – "are called *Adam*," and man alone is not complete.

The talmudic source cited above, goes on to describe life together as a precondition for intellectual-spiritual development, and the meaning of life itself, similar to the *midrash*: "Every man that is without a wife dwells without joy, without blessing, without good[…]. In Palestine they say: Without Torah, without wisdom" (*Yevamot* 62b).

The Babylonians, according to this text, valued marriage highly, attributing great virtues to it, and the lack of these virtues to one who is guilty of the sin of bachelorhood. As further support for their assertion, they cite the words of the Rabbis of *Eretz Yisrael*, who believed that knowledge of the Torah and intellectual development also depend upon marriage. A man requires his wife's support in order to acquire Torah knowledge and attain intellectual development.

The idea that man, woman and God join together to form a single whole can be summed up in the words of Rabbi Akiva to Rabbi Ishmael in the *Midrash*: "Neither man without woman nor woman without man nor both of them without the *Shekhinah*" (*Midrash Rabbah* Gen 22, 2).

This midrashic source is interesting and unusual in that it emphasizes reciprocity: Most of the sources we have cited, refer only to the man – the deficiencies of his bachelorhood, the great good he can expect if he marries, and his lack of prospects if he fails to marry. Rabbi Akiva notes the need of both – "neither man without woman," immediately followed by "nor woman without man." Neither can be complete in her/his personality without the other. The meaning of the togetherness they share, if it is a deep and real bond, will transform the two-way relationship into a three-way relationship: "nor both of them without the *Shekhinah*." There are those who assert that the absence of the *Shekhinah* will cancel "both of them," i.e., their relationship, while its presence will uphold it. Others understand that the presence of the *Shekhinah* depends on both of them: If they are together in every sense, the *Shekhinah* will necessarily be together with them. "And a threefold cord is not quickly broken" (Ecc 4:12). Such descriptions of reciprocity in relationships between men and women take on even greater prominence in light of the fact that we have stressed a number of times here, i.e., that we are dealing with texts "written by men and for men."

The dominant approach in the Talmud, whereby human perfection is manifested in the union of the sexes, creates a certain linguistic difficulty, since the Hebrew word "*Adam*" is used to express both "man" and the unity created by the joining of man and woman: "Rabbi Eleazar said: A man (*adam*) who has no wife is not a man, as it is written: 'Male and female created he them … and called their name Adam'(Gen 5:2)" (*Yevamot* 63a).

"*Adam*" is the common name shared by man and woman, who in their unified creation constituted one whole, as we have seen in the rabbinic versions of the myth of androgynous creation. They were created as a single whole, and it is to this whole that they must strive to return throughout their lives. This idea appears above in a similar statement ascribed in *Midrash Rabbah* to Rabbi Hiya bar Gamda. Rabbi Eleazar goes a step further than Bar Gamda however, asserting that a man who has no wife is not only "unwhole," but does not even merit the name "*adam.*" Man is worthy of being called "*adam*" only when he has a wife – as God called them *Adam* only after he had created them male and female.

The systematic, deep-seated and complex approach developed by the Rabbis, based on the belief that the love relationship between men and women is perfection, was not a natural outgrowth of the culture in which they lived and worked or of the social norms of their time. This clearly male-dominated society, which failed to outlaw polygamy, would have had little interest in the far-reaching assertions regarding man's total dependence upon woman, in every aspect of life, including intellectual development. Recognizing their own deficiency and incompleteness without a female partner in their lives, making the achievement of perfection conditional upon marriage, was in fact a tremendous concession in terms of their belief in male superiority and independence. This systematic process laid the foundations for the revolution in the status of women, and the possibility of creating true love relationships between men and women.

5. Conclusion

Feminist innovation and revolution in the canonical sources appear in a number of contexts:

1. Intention to change the social norm with regard to the status of women in the family: A message of monogamy to a polygamous culture. This message appears as a central motif throughout the Bible, and is given practical emphasis in the words of the Talmud and the personal history of many of the talmudic sages.

2. Defining an ideal paradigm for love relationships between men and women: A harmonious approach based on reciprocity and emotional, intellectual and physical attachment. The dichotomous approach has demonized woman as instruments of evil, who by their very presence arouse desire in men. The harmonious approach requires a physical relationship and pleasure from sex within the framework of marriage, and moreover, recognizes a woman's right to enjoy sex, and imposes the duty upon the man, in a special precept, to have sex with her for the sake of pleasure. This approach thus constitutes a gateway to change in the status of women and in men's attitudes toward women in general.

3. Presenting man as a divided, incomplete creature, whose intellectual, moral, spiritual, and certainly physical completion depends upon his female partner and the harmony in their reciprocal relationship. In terms of male society, it is as if the men ceded control over part of their territory, making room for women.

4. Including the gender phenomenon, male and female, in an equal fashion in the concept of "God's image," and later, in divinity itself, affords supreme legitimacy to harmony and reciprocity between the sexes, and serves as a solid ideological and theological basis for change in the status of women.

Without delving into the specific motives behind such innovation in the writings of male authors throughout history, I believe that at the heart of their work lies a moral conviction that refused to accept the social and cultural norm, driving them to lay the foundation for change.

The Educational Process from a Gender Perspective

The Educational Message to Girls and Boys in an Age of Change

BILHA ADMANIT

A number of months ago, I was speaking before a group of 11th grade girls, on the subject of women's *mitzvah* observance in private and in public. A discussion ensued, during the course of which various ideas were raised, for and against, and one of the girls remarked: "It's not enough for you to speak to us. Go speak to the boys, and get them **to agree** to it."

About a month later, I gave a similar talk to a group of boys at a yeshiva high-school in the Jerusalem area. Once again, there was a discussion, and one of the boys said: "Why are you speaking to us. Go talk to the girls, and get them to **want it**."

The different verbs used – the girls having to want it, and the boys having to agree to it – reflect a master-serf relationship. The change in hierarchical relations between them will come, only after the two sides have gone through a process whereby the serf will want to change her status, and the master will agree to accept her as an equal.

Master-serf relationship is perhaps a bit harsh for our times. These two stories however, lead me to treat relations between boys and girls – and by extension, relations between men and women – in terms of majority and minority: women, not as a quantitative minority, but as a minority when it comes to the quality of power –

as opposed to male society, which retains social, cultural and religious control.

That is the way things are, and the question is, will that be the way things will remain?

In view of the fact that we are different, and in view of the fact that society is stratified, it is only natural that circles of influence would develop. In the center is the majority group – in terms of quantity or quality, i.e., relative concentration of power. This group determines the rules of social conduct; the parameters of cultural discourse; and what is correct, accepted, worthy, unusual, fashionable or outdated.

On the other hand, we have the minority group. Members of the minority group sense the difference that makes them a minority, and are aware of the balance of power between them and the majority. According to S. Herman,[1] membership in a minority group in itself usually carries deep psychological significance. Members of the minority group develop their individual and group identities through constant interaction with the majority identity. They do so, in order to develop a significant group affiliation, and come to terms with its positive aspects.

Generally speaking, we can identify three ways in which the minority may act vis-à-vis the majority: The first way is that of rejection or refusal to accept the norms determined by the majority. In such cases, the minority sets itself apart – voluntarily or at times involuntarily – by creating a parallel social system. An example of this is the *haredi* community within Israeli society. This path is not suited to relations between women and men however, as it stands little chance of reversing the historical pattern.

The second way is that of assimilation: gradually and consciously eliminating unique characteristics, while attempting to

---

[1] S. Herman, 1975. *Jewish Identity – A Psycho-Social Perspective*, Zionist Federation, Jerusalem (Hebrew).

maximize integration within the majority group, to the point of complete assimilation. Jewish assimilation throughout history is a typical example. Without entering the debate over gender-related personality traits – congenital or culture-dependent – it seems a reasonable assumption that millennia-old culture-dependent traits will not disappear within a single generation. This path would thus appear to be impractical, at least as an initial process.

The third way is that of interweaving, developing the other perspective, and making it a part of the accepted norm, of equal standing in the social and cultural discourse. I would like to focus on this path, which I believe to be the correct one – as the way in which to integrate a minority within a majority society, without losing the former's unique character.

Hannan Hever,[2] in his article on Arabic literature, describes the process as follows: The minority accepts norms and values of the majority in a selective and controlled manner, but challenges its exclusive authority. The minority identifies weak points in the majority culture, thus forcing the majority to allocate weight and importance to the minority as well. The greater the minority's awareness of its own strength, the greater its ability to be included as a legitimate partner in the social process. Through this interaction, the cultural boundaries of the society are redrawn, and that which was once considered unusual becomes, henceforth, a part of the norm.

In other words, the more active and determined the minority, the more aware of its own strength and ability, the closer it will be to the center, ensuring that its values and cultural heritage are included in the cultural canon of the society as whole.

---

[2] H. Hever, 1989. "Striking Achilles' Heel," *Alpayim* 1 (*Sivan*), 1989, pp. 186–193.

Tova Cohen[3] discusses women Hebrew writers who chose to engage in the development of female creativity, specifically through the use of canonical texts – religious and literary – written by men, and representing the Jewish cultural and intellectual world, the male world. She terms the process "appropriation," i.e., the adoption of the language of male culture, but not as is, rather changing and adapting it to suit the personal expression of the woman writer. By deconstructing the language of male culture and reconstructing it, a renewed cultural canon can develop, one that includes women. This is the path of interweaving, a two-way development, both giving and receiving.

Similarly, we can identify three ways in which the majority may act vis-à-vis the minority: The first is to scorn or disregard the culture represented by the minority, e.g., past attitudes to *mizrahi* culture. The second is to demand and expect the minority to assimilate and become like the majority, e.g., the "melting-pot" policy. The third way is to be willing to engage in dialogue.

Dialogue is defined by Yakov Malkin[4] as something broader than a two-way conversation. In a conversation conducted as debate, the goal is victory and the refutation of the other position; while in conversation conducted as dialogue, the goal is to increase understanding, and to see reality from the other's perspective. Dialogue is not about blurring or fusing identities, but rather about recognizing the mutual contribution of each side, and accepting differing points of view.

In its very willingness to engage in dialogue, the majority concedes its monopoly over establishing the socio-cultural canon, and

---

[3] T. Cohen, 1996. "Inside and Outside Culture: On the Appropriation of the 'Father Tongue' as a Path to the Intellectual Development of Women's Self-Image," in *Studies in Hebrew Literature*, vol. 1, Tel-Aviv University (Hebrew).

[4] Y. Malkin, 1990. *Dialogue*, Jerusalem (Hebrew).

expresses its willingness to make room on the stage of public discourse for a different, minority opinion – for the other. In attempting to determine the source of this willingness and concession, we will find both practical and ethical motives.

One practical reason might be an inability to withstand the social pressure exerted by the minority; fear that intransigence might lead to rebellion or social unrest; or perhaps fear of economic loss, as was the case with women's suffrage.

An ethical reason might be a belief in human dignity, in the idea that the minority is entitled to equal rights and active participation. The majority is aware of its power, and even enjoys its benefits, but is also committed to the value of making room for the other, and perhaps also to the understanding that the stage is broader than a single opinion can define, as comprehensive and extensive as it might be.

Such views may be ethical and fair, but they are still paternalistic – the perfect majority prepared to make room for the minority as well. Is this enough? Is there no other way?

Rabbi Adin Steinsaltz,[5] commenting on Eve, claims that man and woman are components of a single whole. This whole was divided in two at creation, and each side is in effect only a part, half a body seeking its lost other half.

Janine Chanteur, who writes on the history of war in general, asserts: Complete humanity belongs neither to man nor to woman, but is an unattainable ideal. We are all incomplete creatures, and what we are missing is the "other," toward whom we aspire, and who we can never be. There is a kind of ontological rift. That impossible expectation that we will find our missing wholeness in the other is the source of disappointment, frustration, violence and

---

[5] A. Steinsaltz, 1983. *Women in the Bible*, Ministry of Defence, Tel-Aviv (Hebrew).

war.[6] According to Chanteur, a possible remedy for this might be the creation of a new relationship between the sexes, one of dialogue based on mutuality. This relationship recognizes the individual limitations of each "self"/"sex," accepts the fundamental difference between the sexes, and turns it into a source of reconciliation between them, and between human "otherness" in general.

Human history is patriarchal. The process of creating the tools and the content for that other dialogue, that new dialogue between the sexes, is therefore a challenge faced by society as a whole. We must create a dialogue in which women are no longer a minority; in which there is equal value even without equal identity; in which each side understands the range of otherness in her/himself and is aware of her/his own limitations. Building such dialogue and internalizing it are challenges faced by society and education, inasmuch as they are interconnected – for education both shapes and reflects society.

I would like to raise a number of issues that should be emphasized in the educational process:

1. How can men be persuaded to give up their position of power, gained over millennia of social order? How can boys be taught to develop a male identity not necessarily based on power?

2. How can women be persuaded to give up the convenience of not taking public responsibility, i.e., "I love my master; I shall not be free"? Tamar Ross,[7]

---

[6] From Y. Yovel, 13.4.1990. "Gender-Differences as the Root of War," *Ha'aretz* (Hebrew).

[7] T. Ross, 1995. "The Status of Women in Judaism – A Few Remarks on Leibowitz' Views Regarding the Co-ordinating Mechanism between

on the subject of changing the status of women in the religious sphere, claims that change will not come about by constitutional amendment, that is intentional action from above, but rather through a change in consciousness from below. A slow and sincere shift by women toward a more active role in religious life will bring the establishment to take them into consideration. How can this be encouraged?

3. How can we explain both the advantages and disadvantages of the old and new orders respectively? Every path involves give and take and every ideology has its price. Every choice entails cost. We must therefore ask: How can we learn to live with the cost, and how can we minimize it?

4. Sylvia Ann Hewlett writes:[8] "The call to liberation will not have great significance for men or women, if women enter the world of men on their [i.e., men's] own terms." How then can we develop the "Different Voice," to quote Carol Gilligan? How can we make room for it? How can we ensure that it leaves room for others, and does not intimidate?

5. Studies have shown that the entry of women into the professional and educational world has harmed the stability of the family. Is this a necessary outcome, or

---

Halakhah and Reality," in Y. Leibowitz, *Olamo VeHaguto*, edited by A. Sagi.

[8] S.A. Hewlitt, 1986. *A Lesser Life: The Myth of Women's Liberation in America*, William Morrow & Co., New York.

can women be integrated actively and productively into society without or with minimal adverse effect on the family? Ruining the family is a heavy price to pay – is every social achievement worth the cost?

6. How can we make room for women who prefer the old order, and do not want change? How can we make room for recognition and acceptance of other voices among us?

7. How can we create a process of change, while preserving the valuable things the old framework has to offer? How can we avoid indiscriminate destruction? How can we avoid discovering too late that there is no stable structure capable of accommodating the new idea?

8. How can we develop the patience and perseverance required by lengthy social processes? How can we learn to live with unresolved problems? How can we learn to cope, in terms of understanding and empathy, even when there is no possibility of immediate change?

Change also involves exchange. We must understand, learn and teach, that change in relations between the sexes – which some of us are struggling to achieve, and by which others among us feel threatened – does not necessarily mean destroying the existing order and discarding all significance. Within this change also lies the possibility of building another system, with limitations we must learn to recognize, but of no less value than its predecessor.

The processes of construction, study and adaptation are the challenges of today's educational, religious and social systems. As it is written in the book of Hosea (2:18): "And it shall be at that day, saith the Lord, that thou shalt call me 'my husband' (*ishi*); and shalt call me no more 'my master' (*ba'ali*)." This applies to personal relationships between man and woman as couples, as well as to relations between men and women in society in general.

Feminist Currents and Trends Among Various Orthodox Groups

CHANA KEHAT

In approaching the subject of feminism within Orthodoxy, I explored various images of women, within the different Orthodox groups, and discovered that nothing is new. The figures I identified, closely matched the archetypes of women in the ancient traditions of rabbinical literature.

We find today, in Jewish Orthodoxy, at least four paradigms of women, according to group affiliation:

1. The woman who influences and encourages her husband to engage in personal-spiritual development. She forgoes personal fulfillment, shoulders a dual role – that of housewife and of provider – for the sake of her Torah-studying husband and his spiritual development. There no difference between her property and that of her husband, or in the words of Rabbi Akiva, "what is his – is hers." Most *haredi* women and many of those termed "National-*haredi*" belong to this group.

2. The studious-feminist woman. These are women who belong mainly to the Modern Orthodox stream,

which has already produced a generation of Torah-educated women.

3. The militant-feminist woman. This group essentially resembles the Modern Orthodox group. Its roots can be found in American Jewish Orthodoxy, and it is currently gaining popularity among Orthodox women in Israel as well.

4. The woman who lives in the shadow of a man – according to the traditional patriarchal approach. She has no independent status and her voice is not heard. She functions as an object, and is perceived as such.

As I have mentioned, similar categories appear in the midrashic literature, although generally-speaking the prevailing female figure is that of the last group, which represents the majority of women, and which certainly typifies the image of women in most traditional sources. Some texts however, also portray women of the other types listed above:

1. **Rachel, wife of Rabbi Akiva**, is the classic example of a woman who sacrifices herself and her development for the sake of her husband and his Torah study. She perceives herself as his livestock (*rahel* means 'ewe'), while he attributes his success and that of his students to her. This mutual self-effacement shows self-sacrifice and idealism. This is a woman who acts behind the scenes, forgoes her own personal development and attains fulfillment through her husband, whose instrument she is. Rabbi Akiva was a shepherd who worked for Kalba Savu'a. The daughter of the latter observed that he was humble

and capable. She said to him: 'If I marry you, will you
go to the house of study?' He replied that he would.
She married him secretly, and sent him off to study.
Her father found out, threw her out of the house,
and abandoned her to poverty. Akiva spent twelve
years at the house of study. When he returned, he
was accompanied by 12,000 students. He overheard
a certain old man say to Rachel: 'how long will you
act as a living widow?' She replied: 'Were my husband to listen to me, he would remain in the house
of study for another twelve years. Rabbi Akiva said, I
have her permission, and returned for another twelve
years. When he came home, he was accompanied by
24,000 students. His wife heard of his return and
went out to greet him. Her neighbors urged her to
borrow some clothes to wear. She said: "A righteous
man knoweth the life of his beast" (Prov 12:10).
When she came before Rabbi Akiva, she prostrated
herself and began to kiss his feet. His attendant
pushed her away, and Rabbi Akiva said: 'Let her be.
What is mine and what is yours is hers' (*Ketubot* 62b–
63a).

2. **Beruriah** represents the second figure, the studious-
feminist, who resembles male scholars in her abilities
and achievements. According to legend, Beruriah,
the wife of Rabbi Meir, was a true scholar, of greater
fortitude than her husband, greater understanding,
greater sensitivity and greater wisdom, who succeeded in realizing her full potential. Although Rashi

asserts that she came to a bitter end, Daniel Boyarin[1] has proven that this legend has no traditional historical basis. This is the paradigm of the new religious girl – studious and revolutionary, but also faithful to tradition. The following are a number of passages describing the figure of Beruriah:

"Beruriah, the wife of Rabbi Meir, daughter of Rabbi Hananiah ben Teradion, was accustomed to learn three hundred lessons a day, from three hundred sages, and even so failed to complete the task in three years" (Pesahim 62b).

"Certain outlaws living in Rabbi Meir's neighborhood used to harass him. Rabbi Meir prayed for mercy for himself, and for their deaths. Beruriah his wife said to him: 'Are you relying on the verse 'Let the sins be consumed out of the earth' (Ps 104:35)? It doesn't say 'sinners' (*hot'im*). It says 'sins' (*hata'im*). Furthermore, go to the end of the verse, where it says 'and let the wicked be no more.' Let the sins be consumed – and the wicked will be no more? Pray for their repentance, and 'the wicked will be no more.' And indeed he prayed for mercy upon them, and they repented" (*Berakhot* 10a).

"Rabbi Yose the Galilean was on the road, when he met Beruriah. He asked her: 'By which road should we travel to Lydda?' She replied: 'Galilean fool, did not the rabbis say 'Talk not overmuch with women'? You should have asked 'By which to Lydda?' Beruriah found a certain student studying in an undertone. She rebuked him, saying: 'Is it not written 'ordered in all things and sure' (II Sam 23:25)? If the Torah be ordered

[1] D. Boyarin, 1989–90. "Diachrony vs. Synchrony: A Tale of Beruriah," *Jerusalem Studies in Jewish Folklore*, 11–12, pp. 7–17.

in the two hundred and forty-eight organs of your body, it will be sure, and if not, it will not be sure" (*Eruvin* 53b–54a).

"From what point can an oven become impure? From the time it is stoked for baking [...] Rabbi Halafta of Kefar Hananiah said: I asked Shimon ben Hananiah, who asked the son of Rabbi Hananiah ben Teradion, and he said from the time it is moved from its place, and his daughter said from the time its attachment is severed. Rabbi Yehudah ben Bava said: His daughter has spoken better than his son" (*Kelim Kama* 4, 9).

"Who can find a virtuous woman? A story is told of Rabbi Meir, who was sitting and teaching in the house of study on a Sabbath afternoon, when his two sons died. What did their mother do? She lay them both down on the bed and covered them with a sheet. After the Sabbath was over, Rabbi Meir returned from the house of study to his home, and asked her: 'Where are my two sons?' She said they had gone to the house of study. He said to her: 'I waited at the house of study, but did not see them.' He was given a cup for the *havdalah* service, and he recited it. Again he asked: 'Where are my two sons?' She replied that they had gone elsewhere, and that they were now returning. She gave him something to eat and recited the blessing. After he had recited the blessing she said to him: 'Rabbi, I have a question to ask you.' He told her to ask. She said: 'Earlier, a man came and gave me something for safekeeping, and now he has come to take it. Shall we return it to him or not?' He said to her: 'My daughter, One who holds something for another must return it to its owner.' She said: 'Rabbi, without your approval, I would not have returned it.' She then took him by the hand up to the room, brought him close to the bed, removed the sheet, and he saw the two boys lying dead on the bed. He began to weep, crying: 'My sons, my sons! My

teachers, my teachers! My sons they were, and my teachers as
well, for they would light up my face with their Torah-study.'
She then said to Rabbi Meir: 'Rabbi, that is not what you told
me. You said that a man must return something he is holding
for another to its owner.' He said: 'The Lord gave, and the
Lord hath taken away; blessed be the name of the Lord (Job
1:21). Rabbi Hananiah said that he was comforted by this, and
that is the meaning of 'Who can find a virtuous woman?' "
(*Midrash* on Prov 31:1).

3. **Yalta** represents the figure of the militant Orthodox
woman. Yalta, wife of Rabbi Nahman, was, according to the texts, rich, wise and a militant feminist.
Her demands pertained both to matters of status and
religion:

"Ulla came to the house of Rabbi Nahman, ate bread, recited Grace after Meals and gave the cup over which the
blessing had been recited to Rabbi Nahman. Rabbi Nahman
said to him to send the cup to Yalta. Ulla replied that there was
no need to do so, for Rabbi Yohanan had said: 'The fruit of a
woman's body receives blessing only from the fruit of a man's
body, as it is written: 'he will also bless the fruit of thy body'
(Deut 7:13) – it does not say 'the fruit of her body,' but 'the
fruit of thy body.' Yalta heard, and being the daughter of the
exilarch, was not accustomed to being scorned. In her anger
she went down to the wine cellar and broke four hundred
barrels of wine. Rabbi Nahman later asked Ulla to send her
another cup. Ulla sent a message to Yalta, saying: 'This entire
barrel is a barrel of blessing, and even if you do not drink from
the cup of blessing itself, you may drink wine from the entire
barrel.' She sent him back insulting words: 'Gossip comes from
peddlers, and lice from rags' " (*Berakhot* 51b).

These two expressions may be referring to Ulla himself, who used to travel between Babylon and *Eretz Yisrael*, and to his chatter. His words are chatter, because his claim is incorrect. It is not true that the entire barrel was a 'barrel of blessing,' since only the cup over which the blessing was recited is a 'cup of blessing,' and his attempt to placate Yalta by fooling her is unsuccessful. As a stranger in town, the fact that he spoke ill of women while in Yalta's house shows how little he understood of the place and circumstances. Had he realized how important a woman Yalta was, he would have been wary of offending her by saying the things that he said about women. The criticism here is twofold. The strange statement 'and lice come from rags' may be an expression of contempt for his assertion that a woman is only blessed by the fruit of her husband's belly. In disregarding the status and importance of women, he is like a rag in which lice develop, since the Rabbis believed that lice reproduce asexually.

4. **The women of ...** These women have no names. They are the ordinary women, described as temptresses, demanding physical pleasures and leading men into evil. These women usually complain about material things and a lack of respect. They are often the object of harsh words and well-known stereotypes. There is a relatively large number of negative descriptions of them, emphasizing their lack of individual identity and general inferiority: "Women have four characteristics. They are gluttonous, inquisitive, envious and indolent."[2] "A woman is like an unfinished vessel, and does not enter into a covenant ex-

---

[2] *Midrash Rabbah, Devarim* 6.

cept with the one who makes her complete."[3] There are also examples of specific women belonging to this group:

The wife of Rabbi Gamliel:

"When Rabbi Akiva made a city of gold for his wife, Rabbi Gamliel's wife was jealous, and became angry with her husband. She told him of the matter, and he said to her: 'Have you done for me what she has done for him? She sold the plaits of her hair for him, and he went to study Torah for twenty-eight years" (JT *Shabbat* 6, 1).

The wife of Rabbi Yohanan ben Zakai:

"Hanina ben Dosa went to study Torah with Rabbi Yohanan ben Zakai; and Rabbi Yohanan ben Zakai's son fell ill. He said to him: 'Hanina, my son, pray for him, that he might live.' He put his head between his knees and prayed for him, and he lived. Rabbi Yohanan ben Zakai said: 'Had Ben Zakai put his head between his knees the entire day, he would not have been answered.' His wife said to him: 'Is Hanina greater than you?' He replied: 'No, rather he is like a slave before the king, and I am like a minister before the king" (*Berakhot* 34b).

The wife of Rabbi Hanina ben Dosa:

"Every Sabbath eve, Rabbi Hanina's wife used to warm up the empty oven, out of shame [...] Rabbi Hanina's wife said to him: 'How much longer will we suffer in our poverty?' He said: 'What shall we do?' She said: 'Pray to God that he might give you something.' He prayed and a sort of hand came out and gave him the leg of a golden table. In a dream he saw all of the righteous in Paradise sitting and eating at a golden table with

---

[3] *Sanhedrin* 22b.

three legs, and they were sitting at a table with two legs. He said to her: 'Are you happy that all of the righteous are sitting at a table with three legs, and we are sitting at a table missing one leg?' She said to him: 'What shall we do? Pray that it be taken back.' He prayed, and it was taken" (*Ta'anit* 25a).

What are the reasons behind the different development of each group of women?

The different feminist trends within Orthodox Judaism should be viewed and analyzed using a three-dimensional system: First, the reference group, comprising many and varied sub-groups; second, the level of feminist consciousness; and third, the areas in which feminist development are expressed.

1. The reference group.

This group possesses a complex system of fundamental religious and social values, including a number of variables bearing directly on the feminist changes that will occur within the group. The situation, status and development of the women reflect their social stratum.

The many faces of Orthodoxy in Israel and abroad are reflected in different existential and ideological foundations, as well as a basic life experience that varies from group to group. There are those for whom religion is founded upon "commitment." For some, it is "personal-existential meaning," while for others, the basis of religion is group affiliation. In terms of points of reference and identification, there is a significant difference between Israel and the Diaspora, with further differences apparent between the various sub-groups.

In Israel: In Orthodox society in general, for various reasons, Torah study has become a supreme value in all groups – *mitnagdim*, *hasidim*, modern and *mizrahim*. The measure of social status and success is the extent of Torah study, or in other words, the level of Torah scholarship. In Israel, the need to belong to a synagogue is not perceived to any significant degree as a religious-existential experience.

In the **Diaspora** on the other hand, alongside the value of Torah study, there is greater social regard for other achievements, such as economic success. In addition, living in the Diaspora, within a multi-ethnic and pluralistic society, one feels the need for an identity-oriented framework. In Jewish society, that is synagogue membership. Ethnic origin in Israel, based on the Diaspora experience, is also reflected in synagogue membership. In both places, there are hasidic courts.

This distinction offers a good explanation of the differences between feminist development in Israel and abroad: In Israel, the main area of development among Orthodox girls is that of Torah study, while in the Diaspora, great efforts have been invested over many years in developing a better alternative for women's prayer in the synagogue.

Segregation of the sexes has also had a significant influence on the nature of women's development. Segregated societies, such as the ultra-Orthodox, afford women room for social development, and they do not feel frustrated. It is perhaps for this reason that we see little sign of feminist revolution in *haredi* society today. It is a complete society in its own right, with its own culture, social stratification, etc., in which women do not even come to the synagogue. To a certain extent, this factor also influences the desire, or lack of desire, to be like the men or to create a unique religious path (in this there is an interesting similarity between religious post-feminists who insist upon a consciously unique character for ceremonies in which women take part, and the ultra-Orthodox women – like the resemblance between post-feminists and non-feminists, who advocate a unique women's culture). The Orthodox feminists on the other hand, strive to emulate the men. These subtle differences can be observed in the women's seminaries.

There are also general social factors that create "pseudo-feminist" processes, which in effect have other causes, as in the case of *haredi* women who have become providers, due to current circumstances within their society. Another example of this is the growing political influence of Shas, which relies on mass support, including that of women – a fact that has indirectly provided channels of expression for women, although barred from active participation in politics, and unable to serve as public officials.

2. The level of feminist consciousness.

This is another significant factor in distinguishing between the groups. A high level of consciousness is typical of the Modern Orthodox: liberal and academic for the most part. The conscious feminist struggle of different women's groups has resulted in many and varied changes. Change has also resulted in other groups, but not as a result of a conscious effort. Among the Modern Orthodox, significant weight is given to the "personal significance" of religion, in keeping with modern western thought; as opposed to the ultra-Orthodox or national-Orthodox approach that sees "commitment" as the basis for religious experience. The "commitment" approach precludes taking a critical stance toward tradition – which includes patriarchal elements, and sanctions the continued existence of society as non-egalitarian and hierarchical. Feminist theological discourse is the province of Orthodox academics, capable of living with ambivalent and complex faith systems.

3. Areas of life which reflect feminist processes.

The factors presented above create very interesting variations and changes, and affect many aspects of life: **Behavioral norms** – individual and family lifestyle. **Religious fulfillment**, such as Torah study, observance of commandments from which women are exempt, and participation in religious ceremonies. **Social stratification** – involvement, status and leadership. **Status within the family** – the ability to make choices and decisions, and the extent of equality in household responsibilities. The factors affecting the level of feminism in Orthodox sub-groups can be placed along a scale, with the ultra-Orthodox approach at one end, and the Modern Orthodox approach at the other.

In *haredi* society, Torah study is the supreme value, but feminist consciousness is extremely low – as a result of cultural insularity, as well as an existential religious experience based on commitment to the religious ideal and rejection of the desire for self-fulfillment. Women therefore do not take part in Torah study, but serve the ideal by serving a husband who engages in study; committing themselves to work, thus enabling him to study without the burden of having to earn a living. They participate in religious ritual. Since *haredi* society is segregated however, the women create an independent sub-society, with its own social stratification. There is little feminist frustration, because the women make no attempt to gain social parity with the men, and women's society creates unique areas of culture and fulfillment, such as: good works, avoiding gossip, modesty, and having many children. There is a clear hierarchy within the family. The man is "head of the family," but the woman who goes out to work obtains informal power as the provider. The woman usually plays a dual role, particularly when the family is large: taking care of the children and the home, as well as working outside the home. Rachel, wife of Rabbi Akiva is the paradigm. Circumstances are not as difficult among *haredim* in the Diaspora and within the hasidic community, where the men also work and women are not the sole providers.

Somewhere in the middle are women identified with *Yeshivat Merkaz Harav*, i.e., national-*haredi*. Segregation between the sexes is not complete, and religious meaning lies somewhere between commitment and self-fulfillment. The frame of reference is the *yeshivah*, and feminist consciousness is low, because this is a society that views the religious-*haredi* model as the ideal, and strives to emulate it in many different ways. One of these ways is the empowerment of the male rabbinical leadership, resulting in a paternalistic society. These factors are reflected in the fact that women belonging to this group aspire to religious self-fulfillment, but not in those areas reserved for men. That is why they do not study *Gemara*. These women to not seek change in public ritual, or involvement in religious leadership. On the other hand, unlike women in *haredi* society, they study a good deal of material pertaining to faith and ethics, while accepting male patronage and instruction. In social terms, gender-based differences in status are quite visible, due to the fact that this society is not completely segregated. The potential for comparison and feelings of discrimination are therefore ever present. I believe this society is moving toward greater acceptance of the ideal represented by Rachel, Rabbi Akiva's wife, and the women of this group increasingly resemble *haredi* women.

Generally speaking, Modern Orthodox women fall into two categories: those who live in Israel, and those who live in the Diaspora. In Israel, the past decade has witnessed impressive development among women in the field of Torah study, particular to this country, in which Torah study has become a supreme value. This progress has left its mark on personal behavior, greater autonomy, and the pursuit of Torah-oriented careers (scholars and lecturers in Jewish studies, rabbinical court advocates, halakhic advisors, etc.). The role model for this group is Beruriah.[4] Modern Orthodox women in the Diaspora also live in a mixed society. They identify as militant feminists, and view this issue as a cardinal one, particularly in the context of the surrounding liberal democratic culture (in the United States and Western Europe for example). They demand a role in religious ritual and in the rabbinical leadership: women's prayer groups, Torah-reading, and inclusion in the hierarchy of the general leadership. Yalta, the wife of Rabbi Nahman, in her struggle for the right to receive her share in the "cup of blessing," personifies this type.

---

[4] The first Israeli women's seminary dedicated entirely to Torah study, was called Michlelet Bruria. The name was later changed to Midreshet Lindenbaum.

CONTRIBUTORS

Bilha Admanit, Talpiot – Academic College of Education, Tel Aviv and Yaacov Herzog College, Alon Shevut.

Prof. Tova Cohen, Department, of Literature of the Jewish People and Chair of the Rachel and J.L. Gewurz Center for Gender Research, Bar-Ilan University.

Prof. Rachel Elior, John and Golda Cohen Chair of Jewish Philosophy, Dept. of Jewish Thought, the Hebrew University of Jerusalem; The Van Leer Jerusalem Institute.

Dr. Orit Kamir, Faculty of Law, the Hebrew University of Jerusalem.

Chana Kehat, Chairperson of Kolech – Religous Women's Forum.

Prof. Rabbi Naftali Rothenberg, Senior Fellow at The Van Leer Jerusalem Institute; Rabbi of Har Adar.

Prof. Chana Safrai, the Hebrew University of Jerusalem and Advanced Studies, Hartman Institute, Jerusalem.

Lea Shakdiel, Educator and Social Activist, Yeruham.

Prof. Pinhas Shifman, Faculty of Law, the Hebrew University of Jerusalem.

Susan Weiss, Lawyer, Director of Yad L'Isha, the Max Morrison Legal Aid Center and Hotline, under the auspices of Ohr Torah Stone, research fellow at Hartman Institute, Jerusalem.

Dr. Deborah Weissman, Director of the Kerem Institute for Teacher Training in Jerusalem, is one of the founding members of Kolech, the religious feminist organization in Israel.